THE CENTRALITY
OF
THE CROSS

D0808910

THE CENTRALITY
OF
THE CROSS

Notes of Addresses on the Finished Work of
Christ at Calvary; incorporating "The Logos of
the Cross."

BY

JESSIE PENN-LEWIS

CHRISTIAN • LITERATURE • CRUSADE
Fort Washington, Pennsylvania 19034

CHRISTIAN LITERATURE CRUSADE

U.S.A.
P.O. Box 1449, Fort Washington, PA 19034

GREAT BRITAIN
51 The Dean, Alresford, Hants., SO24 9BJ

AUSTRALIA
P.O. Box 91, Pennant Hills, N.S.W. 2120

NEW ZEALAND
10 MacArthur Street, Feilding

ISBN 0-87508-939-9

First American edition 1993
This printing 1996

PRINTED IN THE UNITED STATES OF AMERICA

"The Greek word used by Paul in First Corinthians 1:18 is *logos . . .*" [not] 'preaching' but "the *subject matter* of preaching; with the *very essence* of that which was to be preached; with that 'Logos' of the Cross which constituted its rationale, its Divine reason, a reason which . . . he declares to be 'the wisdom of God.' . . .

"This *'Logos of the Cross'* is conceived by Paul to be the key which unlocks the riddle of the universe, solves all mysteries, and reconciles all things. . . ."

Henry C. Mabie

CONTENTS

Chapter   Page

1. The Centrality of the Cross 9

2. The Changed Center Through
   the Cross 23

3. The Changed Outlook Through
   the Cross 35

4. The Pathway of the Cross 41

5. The Life-side of the Cross 57

6. The Cross and Life in the Spirit 73

7. The Cross and Power for Service . . . 89

8. The Cross and the Tongue 109

9. The Cross and Revival 115

10. The Cross as a Proclamation 127

Appendix:
The Cross and the Blood Compared . . . 139

Note: The quotations from St. Paul's Epistles are mostly taken from Conybeare and Howson's *Epistles of St. Paul.*

1

THE CENTRALITY OF THE CROSS

LET us turn first to Romans 4:25, to the declared fact of the atoning death of Christ. I was struck in looking lately at Dr. Forsyth's book on "The Cruciality of the Cross," in which he says, "A true grasp of the Atonement meets the age in its *need of a center*, of an authority, or a creative force, a guiding line and a final goal. IT MEETS OUR LACK OF A FIXED POINT." This is exactly the case. We need a "fixed point," which acts as a center and a goal, and that "point" in the history of the world—back to the ages before it, and forward to the ages following it—is the cross of Calvary. It is the central pivot of the dealing of God with the universe in every aspect.

It is because we Christians get away from the "fixed point" of the cross that we wander into all kinds of cul-de-sac places, where we lose the balance and right perspective of truth. At this opening meeting we will gather around this fixed point—the cross of Christ—so that we may get to know more of the Christ of the cross. From this the Holy Spirit will enable us to open up other aspects of truth in their relationship to the cross.

Let us begin at Romans 4:25 (Conybeare's translation), which reads thus: ". . . our Lord Jesus; who was *given up to death* for our transgressions, and raised again to life for our justification." Throughout the Epistles of Paul we find this truth repeated again and again. The death of the Lord Jesus Christ was *a substitutionary and a propitiatory sacrifice.*

The cross is therefore central for the forgiveness of sins and for the justification of the sinner.

Again read Romans 5:6–8: "While we were yet helpless [in our sins], Christ at the appointed time died for sinners. Now hardly for a righteous man will any be found to die (although some perchance would endure death for the good), but God gives proof of His own love to us because, while we were yet sinners, Christ DIED FOR US." Then in verse 9: "Much more, now that we have been justified in His blood,[1] shall we be saved through Him from the wrath of God. For if, when we were His enemies, we were reconciled to God by the DEATH of His Son, much more being already reconciled, shall we be saved by SHARING HIS LIFE."

The words are so plain and obvious in their meaning that, to an open mind, it is *clear* that Christ died *for* us; that we are "justified in His blood"; that when we were enemies we were "reconciled to God by the death of His Son" and, being reconciled, we are saved by "sharing in His life." These are declared basic facts, showing that Christ's death on Calvary was a death for sinners, and produced a reconciliation with God of sinners in a state of enmity against Him. Yes, a salvation for those sinners through the impartation of a "share" of the life which Christ, as their Substitute, obtained for them out of His death.

Now let us pass on to see the cross as the center or "fixed point" for victory over sin, over the world, over the flesh, and over the devil.

For a clear unveiling of the cross as the "fixed point" for the Christian's VICTORY OVER SIN, we turn to Romans 6. This is the basic chapter of the New Testament where the deep meaning of the death at Calvary is set forth, in language which is extraordinary in its simplicity and clearness and marvelous in its comprehensive explanation of the gospel. No wonder that the "god of this world" has influenced so many to relegate Romans 6 to the theologians, so as to keep believers from understanding its simple truth—because the deceiver knows it to be the CRUCIAL MESSAGE OF THE CROSS from the experiential standpoint.

Godward, the death of the Lord Jesus Christ was the atonement, and the propitiation for sin, but in Romans 6 we are shown the cross in its manward aspect—in its dealing with the sinner. Here is the practical, deep and vital message to the sinner, showing him the way of deliverance from the power of sin, from the world, the flesh and the devil. Here in the Romans 6 message of Calvary, Paul laid the foundation deep and strong. Here lies the bedrock depth of the cross, as the "fixed point" for the personal life of the believer—his personal equipment for personal victory in every aspect of need.

Let us read the passage slowly and carefully: Verses 1–2, *"What shall we say then? Shall we persist in sin that the gift of grace may be more abundant?* God forbid! WE WHO HAVE DIED TO SIN. . . ."* Here is the cross in its aspect of the death of the sinner with the Saviour. It is clear from this that Christ's cross was the sinner's cross; not, of course, in the matter of atonement Godward, but in the taking of the old-creation life to the cross so that the believer could be delivered from the power of sin—and that, not by conquering it but by *dying* to it. Here is the key to victory. The deepest things are the simplest.

The real trouble about understanding the sixth of Romans is not a theological but a moral one. When we sincerely *want* deliverance from the power of sin, it is within our reach. It lies just here for the simple soul who will take the statements as a fact. For the sake of a lost world, let us have no "moral" hindrances to our knowing the reality of the cross. If men and women would be utterly willing for the deepest work of the cross to be wrought in or applied to them, there would be a trembling of the powers of hell, a shaking of the kingdom of darkness. The pivotal secret of God's plan for the redemption of a lost world lies in the meaning of Romans 6. The central fact is that the cross is the sinner's cross, as well as the Saviour's.

Moreover, this Romans 6 meaning of the cross must be recognized as the root foundation of the Christian life, just as a good root structure is necessary to the life of a tree. A tree cannot part with its root but must strike it deeper into the ground, so that all its external growth may have strong support in the earth, with a strong life-force for its maintenance.

"We who have died to sin," how can we any longer live under the mastery of sin? Or "have you forgotten that all of us . . . were baptized into fellowship with His death?" writes the apostle. *"All of us"*—not the few who wish to be advanced souls, but young converts also! If every convert to Christ who was "born again" through the gospel message of this chapter knew its power in experience at the very beginning of his or her Christian life, there would be less backsliding, and less need of careful nursing lest they fall away—for a new life would be imparted to them in stronger power, and Christ as the Living One would be known as a real Saviour.

I saw this in Finland some years ago, when the daughter of a professor sat in the front row of the Conference meetings. I was speaking (by translation into Finnish and Swedish) on the corn of wheat falling into the ground to die. There were delegates from all parts of Finland there. The occasion was such that I sought to make the most of my rare opportunity, and so I opened out all that I knew of the deeper meaning of the cross. Someone said, "Will you speak to that girl; she is unconverted." I said, "No, not today. I will wait!" At the end of the third day, when the people were leaving, the girl came along, flung her arms around my neck, and burst into tears. I said, "What is it, dear? Have you come to Christ?" "Yes, I have." "Thank God! What did you see that led you to Him?" And she replied, "The corn of wheat falling into the ground to die." She was born again through this revelation by the Spirit of God, that "when Christ went to Calvary, He took the sinner too." The result was that this soul became more "full grown" in three months than the majority of Christians we meet today. When she was only three months old as a Christian, she was able to translate into Swedish (and to make arrangements for the publishing thereof) the whole of the book *The Cross of Calvary*, and to do it intelligently and fully. This shows us what sort of converts they had in Pentecostal days. They were "born" in Paul's time on the truths of Romans 6.

Let us read the passage again: "*We who have died to sin* . . . or have you forgotten that all of us, when we were baptized into fellowship with Christ Jesus, were baptized into fellowship with His death? With Him therefore we were buried by the baptism wherein we *shared His death;* that even as Christ was raised up from the dead by the glory of the Father, so we likewise might walk in newness of life." Now listen carefully to the next words: "For *if we have been grafted* into the likeness of His *death*, so shall we also *share* His resurrection."

Note the repetition of the words about the cross, making it the "fixed point" of the message. *"We who died"*—Calvary! *"His death"*—

Calvary! *"Shared His death"*—Calvary! *"Grafted into . . . His death"*—Calvary! And again in verses 6 and 8, *"Crucified* with Christ"—Calvary! "Shared the *death of Christ"*—Calvary! How clear it is. *The cross of Christ is the sinner's cross.* And why? Because the whole Adam-life of nature is absolutely fallen. It cannot be improved. It is fallen and poisoned by the Serpent in root and branch. The whole scheme of redemption lies in the fact that God must begin again, so to speak, and make a new creation. Through the cross He plans to bring to an end the old Adam-life of the fallen race, and build again a new creation in the midst of its ruins. There is not even a "divine spark" in the fallen man which He can fan into life as the basis for the new.

This fact is vital for the understanding of God's plan of redemption through His Son's death upon a cross. The devil opposes the doctrine of the Fall, because he knows that if men believe there was no Fall they have no sense of need of the cross. The two hang together. We must therefore be brought by the Holy Spirit to the place where we realize that we have nothing in us that can be "improved," and be willing to come to that cross and to say, "when He went to Calvary, He took the sinner too." Oh defeated child of God, take the simple fact of faith in His words, that *you* died with Christ upon His cross; that *you* were baptized "into His death"— put right into Him, and buried out of sight. And there leave yourself, reckoning that you have died unto sin—and as far as you are concerned, have finished with it. Then reckon upon union with Him in resurrection, *i.e.*, that you have in Him a new life. If we would put it briefly, we might say that when you take the attitude or place of death, God *undertakes to put into you all that He wants out of you.*

What a gospel for the people! Let us give it to them. It is truly a gospel of glad tidings—the cross the place of victory over sin as well as the place of reconciliation with God.

The cross is the "fixed point" for VICTORY OVER THE WORLD. In every one of the Epistles of Paul we find that he refers to the finished work of Christ at Calvary, in one aspect or another. Everything he says in all his letters revolves around the center of the cross. In Galatians, especially, are so many references to the cross in its basal relationship to vital aspects of the Christian life that the epistle might be called the Epistle of the Cross. In Galatians 6:14 we get the strongest passage about the believer's death to the world. The apostle writes about himself, but what was true for Paul is true for us. In this instance Paul saw the "world" in the proselytizing methods of the Judaistic believers, and their desire to escape the persecution of the unbelieving Jews "which Christ bore upon the cross." "But as for me," says the apostle, "far be it from me to boast, save only in the cross of our Lord Jesus Christ; whereby the world is crucified unto me, and I unto the world."

The believer's death with Christ upon His cross therefore means being crucified to the *world* in all its aspects. Not to be a miserable, joyless person, but one filled with the joy and glory of another world. It is not the "cross" that makes us miserable, but the absence of it. It is a delivering cross—a cross that liberates you to have the very foretaste of heaven in you, as already sharers of the power of the age to come. Let each one of us put in our claim for deliverance from the world, so that, as Christians, we do not pander to it, dress like it, act like it, and behave like it. If this message of Calvary was taught and believed, it would end the question of amusements in the church.

Note also that to experience this, it must be a *real* fellowship with Christ in His death. And those who have proved it know that this application of the cross does actually cut you off from the "world"; there is a "gulf" between you and the world, and you can see the people of the world on the other side. Thus looking at the world from the cross, you can go to the world of mankind, "sent" as Christ was sent, to reveal the heart of God—with His compassion of love and His spirit of sacrifice. In going to souls, too, from your place in Christ, you will find yourself alongside of their need, for your own "needs" have been fully met in your union with the risen Lord. Glory to God for the cross that severs us from the world, and the world spirit, and makes a way for us into another world where all is peace and joy and love!

In Galatians, also, we find Paul showing us the cross as THE CENTER OF DELIVERANCE FROM THE RULE OF THE "FLESH." "They who are Christ's have crucified the flesh with its passions and

lusts" (Galatians 5:24). Those who apprehend
this meaning of death with Christ have proved
that it is possible in practice for them to walk
at liberty with no "desires of the flesh" having
mastery over them. In verse 16 of this chapter,
we read of the conflict there is bound to be
between "flesh" and "spirit." Each are essen-
tially opposed the one to the other. When the
spirit dominates, the desires of the flesh are in
abeyance. Verse 24 reveals the secret of this
dominance of the spirit, *as possible through the
cross.* The "flesh" is not to be only kept dormant,
but *"crucified."* This is necessary even concerning
the lawful questions of food and drink. If the
children of God knew this, there would be an
end of dishonor to the Lord's name in their
bondage to "fads" and "fancies," and their
grumbles over the material things concerning
the body. Alas, the "flesh" is pandered to among
God's children in a way that often spoils their
testimony for Christ. Victory in this respect is
also essential in the aggressive warfare against
the powers of darkness, for if the believer is
under *bondage* to a single thing—either lawful
or unlawful to them as children of God—they
are powerless. "They who are Christ's have crucified the flesh, with its passions and its lusts,"
i.e., desires. This deals with "habits" and desires
of the physical nature of every kind. Smoking is
surely one, and the terrible slavery to opiates
and alcohol. It is true that while the "flesh" is to
be crucified in an ethical sense, we do "walk in
the flesh" in a physical and lawful sense; but
even "physically" or "lawfully," the "flesh" is not

to "walk" over us, in any one particular.[2]

Then lastly: THE CROSS AS THE CENTER OF VICTORY OVER SATAN. The passage in the Epistles which shows this clearly is Colossians 2:14–15: "He forgave us all our transgressions, and blotted out the writing against us . . . having taken it out of our way, and nailed it to the cross. And He disarmed the Principalities and the Powers, and put them to open shame, leading them captive in the triumph of Christ." These words take us back to the triumphant statement of our Lord in John 12:31–33, where He said on the eve of the cross, "Now shall the prince of this world be cast out. And I, if I be lifted up from the earth, will draw all men unto Me. This He said, signifying what death He should die." And again, in John 16:8–11, He said, "When He [the Spirit of truth] is come He . . . will convict [RV] the world of sin, of righteousness, and of judgment, . . . of judgment because the prince of this world is [has been] judged." So the Holy Spirit has not only to deal with the soul Godward, convicting it of the sin of not believing God; or manward, convincing him that Christ is his righteousness in the Father's presence—but He has to CONVINCE him of the conquest of his foe at Calvary. This fact is not hidden under ambiguous language in the Word of God. In John 12:31, the Lord states plainly what would occur at the cross, and in John 16:11, He emphasizes and repeats His statement.

THE DEVIL AND ALL HIS HIERARCHIC POWERS WERE DISARMED AT THE PLACE CALLED CALVARY. In the face of all that Satan is doing in the world, and his (apparent) increased power, only the conviction of the Holy Spirit as to Christ's victory at Calvary can keep us in heart rest, and enable us to triumph, and to endure. Moreover, if you *believe* in Christ's victory over Satan, you will find more and more how essential it is that you know the cross to crucify the old Adam-life, so that joined in spirit to the victorious Christ you are lifted above, and enabled to triumph over the foe—and prove that, as far as you are concerned, the prince of this world has been cast out. He is conquered. According to Christ's own words (just refered to), Christ did put him, and all his powers, to an "open shame," just when, in the eyes of the world, they apparently triumphed over Him.

I have only briefly touched upon these four aspects of the cross, to show that it is central in all these things. It is vital and central in connection with justification by faith; vital and central in connection with our victory over sin; vital and central in relation to our personal lives and our external habits; vital and central in connection with victory over our foe. Believers who know these aspects of the cross find themselves standing on the solid foundation of the finished work of Christ, so that all hell cannot shake or overthrow them. However varied their experiences may be, the foundation of God standeth sure. They are on the rock-ground of His finished work at Calvary, comprising not only a complete atonement Godward, but victory and deliverance from the world, the flesh, and the devil. Even though subjectively it may not be wrought out in their experience in all its fullness, they rely upon all its completeness as theirs when they lay hold of any specific aspect in the hour of need. Their faith is in *what Christ has done*, not their experience of it. They know that the "word of the cross . . . is the *dunamis* of God." The full "logos" of the cross—not man's thought of the cross, nor even the preaching of it, but the "word" of the cross itself—the "cross" and all that it involved for Christ and for the sinner; the "Logos of the Cross" as expressing God's inward thought as to the way in which He could deliver fallen man from the results of the Fall and defeat humanity's foe, who, fallen from high estate before him, was the cause of his fall. The fallen Archangel was defeated and the fallen Adam crucified at Calvary.

"This 'Logos of the Cross,'" says Dr. Mabie, "is conceived by Paul to be the key which unlocks the riddle of the universe, solves all mysteries, and reconciles all things," and "to Paul it was given to preach that solvent." The world needs today to know this *"solvent"* of all its mysteries.

Notes

[1] By participation in His blood; that is, being made partakers of His death. *C. and H.* note.

[2] See 2 Corinthians 10:3; and 1 Corinthians 6:12.

2

THE CHANGED CENTER
THROUGH THE CROSS

"If One died for all, then all died [in Him]"
2 Corinthians 5:14

A S we read 2 Corinthians 5:13–18, we cannot
fail to see how deeply, in this passage, the
cross is the very center of the life of the apostle.
We are familiar with the fourteenth verse, which
reads, "For the love of Christ constrains me,
because I thus have judged, that if one died for
all, then all died [in Him], and that He died for
all, that the living might live no longer to themselves but to Him. . . ." These words taken
alone unmistakably teach the identification of
the believer with Christ in His death, and his
emergence into a life where he lives wholly and
entirely unto Christ, and not self. But if the
words are read in connection with the context,
preceding and succeeding verse 14, the veil is
lifted in a remarkable way, showing that verse 14
is the very center of a striking passage, revealing

the circumstances and conditions which brought forth from Paul his reference to the cross.

Let me try to picture the situation behind the words of the apostle. His critics at Corinth were charging him with exalting himself, and being "beside himself" with vanity. But he replies, "If I exalt myself it is for God's cause: if I humble myself, it is for your sakes."[1]

"For *the love of Christ constrains me*" —and then he points to the cross as the reason why he could say this about himself. He knew that *it was not "self exaltation" or vanity manifested in his zeal and intense abandonment to God,* because of his identity with Christ in death. "Self" was no longer the dominant center of his being; "self" was no longer the focal base from which he acted, either in "exaltation" or "humility."

How expressive, in the light of this, are the words of the apostle in verse 16. "We therefore"— here the pronoun, says Conybeare, is emphatic. *"We* therefore view no man carnally," *i.e.*, as you have viewed me. You call me vain and mad in my zeal, but that is a carnal view—the view of the flesh. I know that I have died with Christ, and that I am no longer living unto myself. It is the love of Christ dwelling in me which constrains me. "Whosoever then, is IN CHRIST is a new creation; his old being has passed away . . . all comes out of God . . ." (Conybeare, and Gk. original). "You are calling me mad, and saying this, that and the other about me, but I know it is not "I" which is dominating me, for I have seen the "I" on the cross. I have judged the true meaning of Christ's death. I see that if "One" died for all, then "all died," so that those who are thus "IN Christ" become "new creations." Their center is changed. They have a new center—Christ; all is new and all comes *out of* (Greek *ek*) God, as the central spring of their lives. It is thus that the "love of Christ" is constraining me, bursting out of me like a torrent from the central spring of His life, and not the mere zeal and enthusiasm which you carnally judge to be the power at work in me. . . ."

How in line this is with God's way of revealing the meaning of the cross to His children. The inner knowledge of the cross can never be grasped by the intellect. The death of Christ at Calvary was something so awesome and terribly real that only they who enter experientially into that death can get even a glimpse into it. The message of the cross can never be merely a "doctrine," for it was something more than a "doctrine" to Christ, and, as we see in the life of the apostle of the cross, to *Paul.* God's way of revealing truth is to work it into a man's experience—wrought out in the life, before it can penetrate the intellect. We shall only get Paul's knowledge of the cross as we get Paul's experience, *i.e.,* we must be brought to the same experiential point from which he spoke, if we are to understand his message.

A CHANGE OF CENTER

Now it is the change of *center,* which Paul describes in this passage in Corinthians, which I want to dwell upon for a while. We have spoken of the cross and death to sin, as shown in Romans 6; the cross and death to the world as in Galatians 6; and sometimes of the "grain of wheat" death-life depicted in John 12:24—but we may get light about all these aspects of the cross, and experience a measure of deliverance through the truth, and yet not know deep, deep down in our innermost being this change of the "I" center which the apostle speaks about in 2 Corinthians 5:14. To put it in other words, there is something needing dealing with deeper than "sin" or the "world." It is the selfhood—the "ego"—the "I." Has the cross penetrated *there*? "I," said Paul, "henceforth view no man carnally." When the "I" center is dealt with, the outlook is entirely changed. Even one's "view" of "Christ" can be "carnal"—that is, from the viewpoint of the self-center instead of the "new creation" viewpoint which comes "out of God." It is this bedrock basis of the inner life which we must get down to and examine in the light of the cross. No other way can the Lord set free in us His rivers of living water, nor can we be brought into the place of authority over the powers of darkness, for the selfhood is poisoned at its source by the fallen nature of the first Adam.

Before passing on to further elucidate this from the Scriptures, let me read you a passage from the Appendix to *The Spirit of Christ,* by Dr. Andrew Murray, in which he gives an extract from the writings of Dr. Dorner.[2] He says:

"The character of Christ's substitution is not repressive of personality, but productive. He is not content with the existence in Himself of the fullness of the spiritual life, into which His people are absorbed by faith. . . . Christ's redeeming purpose is directed to the creation, by the Holy Spirit whom He sends, of *new personalities* in whom Christ gains a settled, established being. . . . As a new divine principle, the Holy Spirit creates, though not substantially new *faculties,* a new volition, knowledge, feeling, a new self-consciousness. In brief, He creates a *new person,* dissolving the old union-point of the faculties, and creating a pure union of the same. The new personality is formed in inner resemblance to the Second Adam, on the same family type, so to speak. . . . Through the Holy Spirit the believer has the consciousness of himself as a new man, and the power and living impulse of a new, holy life. . . . Mere passivity and receptiveness are transformed into *spontaneity,* and productiveness. . . ."

Dr. Andrew Murray comments on this:

"This thought that the Spirit of God, as the Spirit of the Divine personality, becomes the life-principle of our personality, is one of extreme solemnity and of infinite fruitfulness. The Spirit not only dwells in me as a *locality,* or within me, alongside and around that inmost Ego in which I am conscious of myself, but, within that 'I,' becomes the new and Divine life-principle of the new personality. The same Spirit that was and is in Christ, His inmost Self, becomes my inmost self. What new meaning it gives to the word, 'He that is joined to the Lord is *one spirit* with Him'! And what force to the question, 'Know ye not that *the Spirit of God* dwelleth in you?' The Holy Spirit is within me as a personal power, with a will and a purpose of His own. As I yield up my personality to His I shall not lose it, but find it renewed and strengthened to its highest capacity. . . ."

Here we have clearly set forth the change of "center" which Paul so acutely realized through the light he had had on the cross.

Three times he affirms this basic "new creation" as his experience.

"I live; *yet not I* . . ." (Galatians 2:20).

"I command; *yet not I,* but the Lord . . ." (1 Corinthians 7:10).

"I labored . . . ; *yet not I.* . ." (1 Corinthians 15:10).

In the church at Corinth, in Paul's words in 1 Corinthians 1:12, we have a glimpse of a contrast to this. "Every one of you saith 'I' . . . 'I' of Paul, 'I' of Apollos. . . ." But Paul did not say "I" in the sense of "I" being the originating and moving spring of his words and actions. "I"— yes, it is "I" still, but a new "I"—a new personality. A new "ego" as Dr. Dorner says—not "Christ and I," with "I" at the center, and Christ, so to speak, by His Spirit alongside of the "I." But a "creation" by the Holy Spirit of a new "I," because of the old "I" nailed to the cross with Christ (Galatians 2:20).

This is something wholly beyond our power to grasp mentally. The "new creation" work must be done by the *Creator* as much as in the first creation in Eden. Let us not be self-deceived and imagine that "not I but Christ" is but a motto, a choice, a purpose. It is that, but far, far more. The Holy Spirit will do His part if we see our need and set ourselves for His deepest work of grace in us.

Here we need to go back to the most vital passage on the meaning of the cross which is to be found in the New Testament. It is part of the great doctrinal Epistle to the Romans, wherein the apostle lays down the foundation truths for the Christian Church upon which alone the whole superstructure of the Christian life can be built.

Passing over the first necessary unfolding of the death of Christ as *Propitiation for sin,* Godward (Romans 3:25), and then as *Substitutionary for the sinner* (Romans 5:6–10), we come to the very bedrock focal point of the sinner's death in the death of his Substitute, in Romans 6. It is the spiritual fact which lay at the base of Paul's words in Galatians 2:20: "I have been crucified with Christ, yet I live, no longer I but Christ lives in me . . ." (*Eng. & Gk. N.T.*). Familiar as we are with the words, and to some extent with the truths of Romans 6, let us take one word only in the chapter, strip it of the context, and through this word see how deep and real the basic central fact of "I" crucified is meant to be. It is the word "dead" in Romans 6:2 (KJV). The Revised Version renders it "died," so as to bring out the aorist tense which is so strongly embodied in it.

The Greek word is "*apothnesko.*" The Greek Lexicon says of this word that it has a prefix "*rendering the verb more vivid and intense, and* representing the action of the simple verb as *consummated and finished.*" It also gives as the meaning of the word, "to *die out,* to expire, to become quite dead."[3]

The same word is used again in verse 7. "He that is *dead* [*apothnesko*] is freed from sin," and verse 8, "If we be *dead* with Christ." Now it is obvious that if Paul used such language of the believer's identification with Christ in His death, he meant something more than a "likeness" or a figure.

Let us for a moment picture the apostle dictating these words to the Romans. We know from other parts of his Epistles how magnificently he would break out with bursts of truth flooding his spirit and mind, as with the very light of heaven. And it was always "truth" revealed by the Spirit in response to need. Here we have Paul dictating his letter. Dealing with the question of "grace" overflowing beyond the deepest depth of the outbreak of sin in the human race, an objection made by Judaizing disputants against his doctrine occurs to him, with the result that there bursts out of his spirit the most wonderful unveiling of the cross. These Jews "argued that if the sin of man called forth so glorious an exhibition of the grace of God," then "the more men sinned, the more God was glorified."[4] But, says the apostle, *the cross deals not only with the sin* but with the *sinner.* Then he bursts out, in vivid and intense language:

"HOW SHALL WE THAT ARE DEAD TO SIN LIVE ANY LONGER THEREIN?"

That is, in Christ's death we have DIED TO SIN, as an act consummated and finished, and he that is thus "dead" is freed from [slavery to] sin (Romans 6:7).

Again let us note that this same word, *apothnesko*, DEAD, is used in 2 Corinthians 5:14, Galatians 2:19 and 21, Colossians 2:20, as well as in Colossians 3:3, "For ye are DEAD. . . ." But let us be careful here. It does not speak at all in these passages of the experiential outworking of the cross, but of a *position* —a central basic position of identification with the death of Christ—which has to be recognized and "reckoned" upon by the believer before the Holy Spirit can do His part of the work. The point I want to press is that all Paul's Epistles, with their marvelous unfoldings of the life of Christ for the Church, had at their base Paul's own personal experience of the "I"—the "self"—crucified, and that we must get to the same basic position as the apostle himself, "I have been crucified with Christ, yet I live, but not I . . ." if we also are to enter into all that the "heavenly life" means experientially.

THE EXPERIENTIAL OUTWORKING

Now having laid the foundation of the need of a new center, of a new creation, a new "ego," so to speak, let us look at a few other passages showing that on the basis of having "died out" to sin, as shown in Romans 6:2, the apostle uses other words to describe the *experiential* outworking of the cross.

In Romans 8:13, he writes, "If ye through the

Spirit do mortify the deeds of the body. . . ." The margin of my King James Version says, "*make to die* the doings of the body." The Greek word used is *thanatoo.* The Greek Lexicon says of this, "to take away the vital principle, the aspect being the lifelessness of that from which the life has been taken away." Here is the work of the Holy Spirit with which the believer has to cooperate. On the faith basis of "dead" (Romans 6:2), the believer must now "make to die" the "deeds" of the body, *i.e.,* yield to the cross all the activity of the fallen nature; and as he does so, *that activity will cease,* for the "cross" deals with the fallen life which energizes the "deeds" incited by it.

There is yet another word used by Paul in the same connection. This is *nekroo,* in Colossians 3:5, in reference to the members of the body. The King James Version says "mortify," the Revised Version margin says "*make dead*"; the Lexicon note is "*to make a dead body or a corpse,* the aspect being toward the corpse and the deed by which it became such," *i.e.,* the "members" of the "body" must be brought in all their actions into harmony with the central fact of "death with Christ." The "members" are to be made "dead," in that they are no longer to be energized by the fallen life of Adam but brought under the power of the cross. They are thereby made "dead to sin" and alive unto God for His service (Romans 6:13).

THE PERPETUAL DEATH-LIFE

And yet there is more. These words "*apothnesko*"

(to die out of sin), "*thanatoo*" (to bring the deeds of the body under the power of that death), "*nekroo*" (to deprive the members of the body of the activity of the old life), do not cover the whole ground. 2 Corinthians 4:10-11 gives another word, showing that there will be no point in our life on earth where the need for the application of the cross will cease. Verse 10 reads in the King James Version, "always bearing out in the body the *dying* of the Lord Jesus." The word dying is *nekrosis*—a "putting to death." The Lexicon says it is "expressive of the action being incomplete and in progress." In verse 11, the word "death" is "*thanatos.*" The deep work of God at the center is but the beginning of all that has to be wrought out in us by the Holy Spirit. How clearly the Greek words used bring out the *position* basis of having "died out" in Christ's death, and the progressive "putting to death" perpetually which must of necessity be done day by day. "In my body I bear about continually the dying of Jesus," writes the apostle, but again the verbal exactitude of the Greek is shown in the use of the word "*thanatos*" (death) in verse 11. The Lexicon says that this describes the cessation of life of any kind. Hence, the "putting to death" of verse 10 to which the believer is always handed over by the Holy Spirit is for the purpose of bringing about the cessation of the activity of the old life of nature—and *this is not once for all, but continuously.* So it just means that from center to circumference, the identification of the believer with Christ in His death is a *necessity* for the growth of the new life at the center into full maturity.

Notes

[1] Verse 13, Conybeare and Howson footnote.

[2] *System of Christian Doctrine.*

[3] These gleanings from the Greek are taken from Bullinger's *Critical Lexicon and Concordance to the English and Greek New Testament.*

[4] Footnote to Conybeare and Howson's translation.

3

THE CHANGED OUTLOOK
THROUGH THE CROSS

2 Corinthians 5:14–16

LET us turn back a moment to 2 Corinthians 5:14–16 (Conybeare): "The love of Christ constrains me, because I have thus judged, that if One died for all, then all died [in Him]. . . . I therefore, from henceforth, view no man carnally; yea, though once my view of Christ was carnal, yet now it is no longer carnal." Here we have the outcome of the changed center in a wholly new point of view, *i.e.*, when the "I" is crucified there is a *changed outlook!* We view no human from the ordinary standpoint of the flesh, for we have exchanged the earthly vision for the vision of God. The Corinthians had charged the apostle with being "mad" in his zeal for God, but his reply shows *how the center-spring made all the difference.* Now turn to the Gospel of John to see that this was the very kind of life lived by Christ when He walked on earth as man.

Let us read first the Lord's words in John 5:19 and 30.

"Verily, verily I say unto you, the Son can do nothing of Himself but what He seeth the Father do. . . ."

"I can of Mine own self do nothing. . . ."

This is the position and privilege which the cross is purposed to bring us into. Not only identification with Christ in His death, as a judicial fact, but a practical life where the "I" is kept in the place of death, so that there results such a union with the risen Lord that moment by moment we rely upon Him as our new center, our source of action—even of speech—as He depended upon His Father, saying, in our measure, as He did, *"I can do nothing of myself."* When Christ is the the center spring of a believer's life, as he is taught of the Spirit he draws upon Him even for words. What a revolution this would make in our conversation and our general tenor of speech.

The "old creation" life is very profuse. But as Christ becomes our center, and the "I" is yielded to the cross, the whole life is brought into light to be placed under His control. Then it is possible that you will become slow of speech, for the knife of the cross deals with the profuse and diffuse language of nature—what we may describe as "unnecessary talk"—and the clamor of earth dies away! You will be willing then to sit in silence when you have nothing to say, and what is more, *you can be still amidst the clamor of tongues,* and be content that you cannot join in the soulish streams of earth.

In the Church of Christ there is a vast amount of infant talk. May the Lord bring us to the cross to have the prattle of the "I" cut down. What shall be done about our speech? Shall we consent to be like John the Baptist, and say "I am a voice"? May the Lord deal with our words. "Let your yea be yea, and your nay, nay, for more than these is of the evil one." The evil one is at work in the old creation life, and he knows how to fan up and inflame floods of speech. But the Lord says "yes" or "no" is enough, if we are relying upon Him to enable us to speak according to His will. Shall we go out of this Conference a more God-controlled people in our words and actions? Shall we choose not to "talk" except as He gives the words, and consent to have the diffuseness of nature's speech taken away? How much better to have but a few words, given in reliance upon God, than to have a flood of empty speech. We need in our Conferences more time to get alone with God, for there is danger in all Conferences of an outpouring of words which almost cloud the light, so that we have scarce time to find Him and hear His voice. Are we willing to be brought to that place where we "cannot do anything" without our God? Where we cannot do anything of ourselves? To lose our "natural" ability, in the sense of using it apart from God? Oh the danger of those who speak on platforms. There is a great difference between handling the sacred Word of God and *the Holy Spirit handling it through us,* and yet we acknowledge that unless God unveils the

Word, our speaking is in vain. The Lord take from us the power to do anything without Him.

"The Son can do nothing of Himself." Let us lay down at the cross our natural abilities, and be willing to really feel these words are true. Then we shall be freed from all pomposity and ostentation in our work, and we shall become simply dependent and helpless, actually relying upon the living Christ every minute. It was Jeremiah who said, "Lord, I cannot speak; I am a child!" In His great grace, the Lord Jesus Christ was a child with His Father in all things. As He moved among men He said, *"I speak not of Myself,"* and He was listening to, and relying upon His Father for judging all things, and all men around Him, all the time. (See John 5:30.) We sorely need that discriminating power. We may know it if we press on to realize that Christ will live in us. To this end let us put aside everything which feeds and strengthens the "I." Because of sin in the mind and will, it is an impossible thing for the *natural* man to have a judgment without a self-bias. But *"My judgment is just"* said the Lord, because He was "judging" in reliance upon His Father. The cry among the people today is for "justice." They crave for righteous judgment. Any man who sees that you have no self-bias in your judgment will trust you. *"My judgment is just."*

Now let us turn to John 7:17.

> *"If any man will do His will he shall know of the doctrine, whether it be of God or whether I speak of Myself. . . ."*

In the light of the theme we are considering, these words are wonderful. See verse 18: "He that speaketh of himself [*from* himself, RV] seeketh his own glory; but He that seeketh His glory that sent Him, the same is true, and no unrighteousness is in Him." This is not only a statement of the Lord's attitude, but it embodies a principle of which, in the believer, the self-center taken to the cross is the key. We know that the Lord Christ spoke the words of God, but He says the attitude of no self-bias is necessary for the *reception* of those words! That is, if any one *wills* to do the will of God without any bias or flinching, then he will prove for himself the divine origin of the Master's words. Any self-originated action has always the "own" as its objective, although it may not appear so. What comes from the "own" seeks the "own," and what comes *from God* seeks God's will always and only, at all times. The self-center taken to the cross for the displacement of the "I" *as the originating spring of actions* in word or deed— this is the principle upon which alone God can reveal Himself and make known His truth to men. In this way, as the Word of God is revealed to us, we can stand unshaken and immovable on that Word as in very deed the Word of God.

Again in John 8:28 we read, "When ye have lifted up the Son of Man, then shall ye know that I AM, and that I do nothing of myself, but as My Father hath taught Me, I speak these things."

Now the question for us is, shall God bring us individually to the bedrock fact of the "I" crucified for Christ to be the new center of our being? Shall He reach the very core, so that "I" shall be recognized by us as displaced and crucified, for the Holy Spirit to recreate and produce a new personality after the pattern of the Man Christ Jesus? Shall we ask Him to do it?

4

THE PATHWAY OF THE CROSS

"Except a grain of wheat fall . . ."
John 12:24 (RV)

NOW we come to the out-working of the cross *subjectively* as a law of life out of death for fruit bearing. We must be brought into a real fellowship with Christ in His death. There is an experiential knowledge of the cross. The Spirit of God applies the death of Christ to us, and then the life-power of the resurrection. He begins at the center, and works out to the circumference. In the pathway of fellowship with His death we learn first the liberation of the spirit, and then find how it works out to the soul realm—that is, in relation to the intellect, the emotions, the dispositions—and then how it works out to the sphere of the body.

But I must point out that although this may be the usual sequence of God's working, He does not always work in this order. Sometimes believers begin at one of the later stages, and then have to be taken back to learn the first elements of truth. Much depends upon their environment, and the knowledge of those who help at the beginning of their Christian life. Moreover, with some the Lord cannot work very quickly. He fits His dealings to the limitation of the soul, and has all kinds of methods and ways of working (1 Corinthians 12:6). Let us not ask Him to put us all in one mold of experience.

Now turn to John 12:24, where we read *"Except a corn of wheat fall into the ground and die, it abideth alone: but if it die, it bringeth forth much fruit."* Then the Lord applied the meaning of this saying of His to the individual disciple, and set forth at the same time a law in the spiritual realm analogous to the law of nature. He said, "He that *loveth his life* shall lose it; and he that *hateth his life* in this world shall keep it unto life eternal. If any man serve Me, let him follow Me . . ." (verses 25–26). This is clearly not the same aspect of the cross as *death to sin.* There is no *gradual* deliverance from sin, no gradual process of death to sin or deliverance from the world, or the flesh. The Spirit of God does not say "A little bit today, and a little bit tomorrow," but to all sin and all workings of the flesh, as soon as you become aware of either— "Drop it!" Romans 6 therefore bids you "reckon" yourself *"dead"* to sin, but John 12:24 speaks of a gradual and progressive law of death in respect to fruitfulness. It speaks not of parting with that which is wrong but with that which is lawful—that which we have by nature—*life.* "Skin for skin, yea, all that a man hath will he give for his life," said Satan to Jehovah about

Job (Job 2:4). It is this "life" which the Lord calls those who follow Him to lay down for His sake, and in fulfillment of the law of death for fruitfulness; *i.e.,* the "life" we have by nature has to go into "death" to enable the "life" of God in us to bring forth fruit.

In verse 25 this is clearly seen in the Greek original, for the two words rendered into English as "life" are not the same in the Greek. One Greek word means the lower form of life, the life of nature—that which we share in common with the animals. The other is the eternal life—the life we have from God in the new birth wherein we are made partakers of the divine nature. The passage could be read thus: "He that loveth his (*psuche,* natural) life shall lose it (*i.e.,* the fruit of it in eternity), and he that hateth his (natural) life in this world shall keep it (*i.e.,* save it from eternal loss) unto life (*zoe*) eternal."

The Lord's children are, to a great extent, mostly concerned with the question of victory over sin, and it is necessary that they should be; but when they know the way of victory over sin, they forget that there is another and deeper phase of the cross beyond that. It is then a question not of sin, but of the *life* by which they live and act. As one has said, the life of nature has no "carrying" power in the spiritual sphere. It has no power of fruitfulness in the spiritual realm. That is why some believers toil so much and get so little fruit. They know victory over sin, but *the life of nature is their animating power in service,* as well as in the ordinary use of their faculties. As a result, their intellect is animated by the life of nature, and their affections and emotions as well. There need not be anything *sinful* in the use of their intellect or affections, but their very "virtues" are from the life of nature, and not from the life of God within them. The life of nature as the animating power in the believer, instead of the life of God, means powerlessness in the spiritual conflict, for a spiritual foe cannot be fought by the "natural" man, with natural weapons. Therefore, insofar as we walk in the life of nature, to that extent we are powerless in the warfare with the powers of darkness. They are supernatural, and can only be met by spiritual power. Even though we may, up to the extent of our consciousness, have victory over known sin, we deeply need to learn the way to "hate" or reject the life of nature, even as the Lord Christ Himself poured out His sinless soul at Calvary.

"If any man serve Me, let him follow Me," said the Lord as He spoke of the spiritual law of life out of death, and the way to lay down the life of nature for the fruitful manifestation of the life of God. At Calvary He committed His *spirit* to God, but poured out His *soul* unto death—even the death of the cross. So the Spirit of God leads us in a path where we, too, pour out our soul-life unto death, in fellowship with the Lord at Calvary. This is the meaning of God taking you in hand and leading you through experiences where you lose all conscious life in the senses; for example, all "conscious" presence of God *in the sense realm.* In such a path it appears at times as if you had lost all your "spiritual" life,

and yet you are able to say, "I am trusting God absolutely, without any emotion, without any consciousness. I am walking in bare faith."

"*I have chosen you that ye should bring forth fruit,*" said the Lord. So in due time, when victory over sin is known, the Holy Spirit leads the soul on into a path where the natural, emotional life subsides, and, in some measure, the active, troublesome, intellectual life loses its power of wasteful activity. He does all this in many different ways with the one who wants to know the fullest life of fruitfulness, and who is willing to follow his Lord as a grain of wheat falling into the ground to die!

Let us think a moment about that picture of the grain, as applied to the believer. The grain may have a beautiful coat, but it is hard. The germ of life is locked up in it. It cannot get out. Locked up in the grain, it produces nothing. The only way to make it fruitful in the production of other grains is to drop it into the dark earth, where it loses its outer shell, its beauty, and even the sunshine and all that made "life" beautiful as it nestled in its place with its companions in the ear of wheat. It loses all as it becomes detached and drops down into the earth. After a time, if you take it up you will find nothing of its polished shell, but there will be a tiny bit of life breaking out. If it is left in the ground to give its life entirely, a new life will later on press through the dark earth back into the sunlight and become an ear of wheat that will ultimately produce fruit, thirty or sixtyfold.

The children of God so often shrink from this

truth of the gospel. They want to be "fruitful," but they are not willing for the way to be made fruitful. They are unwilling to part with this "conscious" or "soul" life in spiritual experience. Let me say, however, that there is a *consciousness in the spirit* which is permanent. The life of God in the spirit has no variations, but spiritual experiences in the "soul" or "natural man" are affected by circumstances and by all kinds of external things. But as the "grain of wheat" falls into the ground to die to all external things, it not only becomes fruitful, but in the believer himself the spirit rises into fuller union with God. Then when the inner spirit-life has become steadfast in God, it moves in the orbit of its path with God, like the planets moving in their orbit in the heavens. This changeless life in God (Colossians 3:3) is never fully known until the believer parts with the activities of the soulish life of nature.

Again, notice in the grain-of-wheat path the law of *increase in fruitfulness.* In the soul realm the believer wins others one by one—a service for God not to be despised or discounted; but when there comes the life of God in us—able to reproduce itself because of the pouring out into death of the soul-life—the law of increase is *one* grain into *thirty,* and each of the thirty again into thirty more. The increase is by *multiplication* apart from the activities of the believer. The life of God in us, set free to act through us as the life of nature is buried in death, quickens everything it touches. One of the old writers describes this life as a "tincture." Take for instance one drop of ink, or a drop of milk, and it will "tincture" a glass of water. Similarly, when the divine life is in the spirit, while the soul-life is being poured out in death, there is a divine "tincture" through the words you speak. Then you may say but a few simple words, *but they bear fruit.* You may do a most ordinary thing, but your simple act leaves an eternal stamp upon the one to whom you did it. Oh, thus to live that everything we say or do has the "tincture" of the life of God in it! That is infinitely more valuable to God and man, and more fruitful for the believer, than the most wonderful "sense" experience, which ends in nothing but the believer's own joy. It makes the "ordinary," everyday life full of God. It is so simple that the one who knows it is so occupied with being "faithful in that which is least" that he does not think whether he is "used" or not. Such a one does not clamor for "power" or for "more power," for he has only to see to the "dying," *i.e.,* the abiding in the death of Christ, while unknown to him the life of God in him is "tincturing" all the "doing," and bringing forth fruit eternal.

"*Bringeth forth much fruit!*" Silently, unobtrusively, the grain-of-wheat life works in the world of men—just in the way that God always works. He does not make any noise over what He does, and does not blow a trumpet telling of what He has done or will do. You ask Him to do something in prayer, but He does not send a message announcing that He is going to do it! It just "happens," as it were, and the world knows nothing about it. Oh the beauty of God's wondrous silent working! Men so like a noise, and a flourish of trumpets. But think of God's weak children in the world as grains of wheat, producing other God-like souls, and affecting the whole world without a noise, just being what they are, and walking with God, with the tincture of God touching everything. Is not this picture more worthy of God, because so opposite to man's way, than something spectacular? There is always some danger about the "wonderful" in believers, because it is liable to be attached to the person. It is so much better that we look "ordinary," even *spiritually*, and very insignificant in our lack of visible "power," while God does His silent working through us in grain-of-wheat fruitfulness, and no glory will ever be attached to us and our personality called "wonderful!"

See now where the *affections* come into this question of the life laid down. It is easier to part with anything than life. "He that *loveth* his life shall lose it"! That means to say, you will get nothing for eternity out of it. You may have victory over sin already, and be happy. That is all right; but he that "loveth his life"—even though he parts with sin—has not got reproducing power, the power to reach others and draw them to the life of heaven. He is clinging to the life that cannot multiply and bring forth fruit for eternity. That is the secret of the lack of multiplying power in the churches everywhere. They cling to the "life"—the soul-life with all its personal desires and personal hope of gain— that cannot multiply.

What then shall we do as we see this? We are

responsible beings. We have a choice. God works on our choices. Say "I choose it. I trust Him to do it." It is very simple. "I choose to surrender my own life to have the other!" Then you will "keep it to life eternal." Make this transaction with God, and then do not flinch or turn back from it, as He leads you on in the way He alone can do. But there is more in it than only the choice of the will. We must go back to Calvary.

Let me turn you again to Romans 6, and in verse 5 you will get the same truth in another form, and more clearly showing how this exchange of life takes place at Calvary. In John 12:24 the Lord was speaking primarily of Himself, but the same law is for both Christ and His members. Let us read Romans 6:5: *"If we have been grafted into the likeness of His death. . . ."* Conybeare's footnote says, "Literally, *have become partakers of a vital union* [as that of a *graft with the tree* into which it is grafted]."

Here again we find the secret of this grain-of-wheat life, definitely in connection with the believer's union with Christ in His death. *"We have been grafted."* Who does the "grafting"? We cannot do it ourselves. It is the work of the Holy Spirit. We are to be grafted into the death of Christ.

What does the gardener do in his work of grafting? He cuts the bark of the stock, slips the graft into its place in the cut bark, binds it up, and leaves the bands there for some time. When he removes them, what has happened? *Tree and graft have become united into one life.* That is exactly what the Holy Spirit has to do for us. We must be grafted into Christ in His death, so that we may live by His life—His Own Risen Life—which He obtained out of death. We must become partakers of a vital union, whereby His life becomes ours, as we lay down the life of nature.

You have another, similar figure in Romans 11:17. *"If some of the branches were broken off, and thou, being a wild olive stock, wast grafted in amongst them, and made to share the root and richness of the olive,"* Paul wrote to the Gentile believers. "Thou wast cut out from that which by *nature* was the wild olive, and wast *grafted against nature* into the fruitful olive" (verse 24). This is so true of the believer spiritually. We are grafted into Christ against nature—*i.e.*, our own nature—so that we may share His Risen life, and live a life on earth which is also "against nature." We are called to live a life on earth that the old "nature" is incapable of living, and we do it by being grafted into Christ, so vitally that we are made to "share the root and the richness" which is ours in Him.

Now let me emphasize the fact that the being grafted into the death of Christ is not a theory. It does not mean that the believer lives by the life of nature and calls it "resurrection life." There are those who are compelled by utter weakness to prove the reality of a true impartation of the life of God. When your very physical life hangs upon your knowing the reality of all this in God, then you know that God is a living God. If the Word of God were not true, and the resurrection power of Christ not a reality, you would not be alive. This is what it means to some to live "against nature," drawing upon the richness of the "olive"—the living Christ.

Briefly, let us now see how this law of *life out of death* penetrated Paul's experience and his writings. If you will ponder over his Epistles in this light you will know the inner life of Paul, and understand the meaning of all that he said and did, because you yourself know something of the life which worked in him. The life of Paul is marvelous—and is possible to every believer who learns its secret. Would to God that out of this Conference God would send some Pauls to labor as he labored, with an utter recklessness of life. "Grafted" into the death of Christ, in very truth, he laid down his life for the brethren. This is within the reach of every one of us. It matters not whether we be old or young, educated or uneducated. It matters not whether we have had a college training or no training, this life out of death can be wrought into us and lived out by us, and we can be fruitful for God wherever we are. No one will quarrel with such a one, because the life is the testimony. Men do not quarrel with the life of Christ lived in and through us in selfless sacrifice. But it requires opened eyes to see how this life can only come to us in and through the death on Calvary; to see life out of death as the law of the universe—the law inwrought as the basic principle of the universe: the law of vicarious sacrifice.

Let us read one of Paul's remarkable pictures of the grain-of-wheat life, as given in 2 Corinthians 4:7–11: "This treasure is lodged in a body of fragile clay, that so the surpassing might, which accomplishes the work, should be God's and not my own. I am hard pressed, yet not crushed; perplexed, yet not despairing; persecuted, yet not forsaken; struck down, yet not destroyed. In my body I bear about continually the dying of Jesus, that in my body the life also of Jesus might be shown forth. . . ." Is not this quite plain? Grafted into the death of Jesus, the believer is daily "given over to death" that the life of Jesus might be manifested. One of the effects of this "death" is that we lose a certain exterior "hardness" which most of us have by nature, as if the clay of the earthen vessel acted as a veil of the true life within. Too often others meet the "clay" exterior and not the life of Jesus within. But as the "grain of wheat" shell is broken away, there comes about a simplicity of manner and absence of reserve which enables the inner life to shine forth and draws others to come to you without fear. Oh how the poor world, and the lonely souls in the church, miss that "tincture" of God through His children. There is a barrier, they say, between employer and employed, but there is also a barrier *between the Christians and the unsaved,* which ought not to be. The persons they want to win they cannot, because of this external "reserve" and shell. They want to shake hands cordially, but they do not know how to do it. Oh that we may be so grafted into the death of Jesus that the very life of Jesus, in His heart-love for souls, can be manifested in us and through us—a heart for all the souls you meet, even the people you do business with every day. A heart which will not allow you to "drive" and "push" them, or to ignore their troubles because you are so concerned with your own.

Is it not wonderful that the Christ of Calvary came and first lived the life He wants us to live? "Christ Jesus being in the form of God thought it not robbery to be equal with God," yet He stripped Himself of His glory, and "took upon Him the form of a *slave,* being changed into the likeness of man." He came and lived it first, and then *through His death,* and our death with Him, He desires to live it all out again in us, saying of the poor, dark world of men, "Through My children they will understand Me, for there is the same spirit in them as there was in Me." We can see now why Paul was able to say, "*I rejoice in the afflictions* which I bear for your sake, and I fill up what yet is lacking of the sufferings of Christ . . . on behalf of the church" (Colossians 1:24); and again in Philippians 2:17–18, "Though my blood be poured forth upon the ministration of your faith, I rejoice for myself, and with you all, and do ye likewise rejoice, both for yourselves and with me." Do you "rejoice" when *others* are poured out *for you* for Christ's sake? "Oh no," you say, "I am willing to be spent, but I do not want anyone to be spent for me!" Ah, but it takes much grace for some independent characters to allow anyone to be "spent out" for *them!* But Paul said, "Though my blood is poured forth, I rejoice . . . and do ye likewise rejoice."

Neither Paul nor others must be robbed of

their fruit, when they desire to *lay down their lives for others*. How it pains when those in need are unwilling to have anything done for them. Take heed lest there be "self" even in this. Christ, for the joy set before Him, endured the cross. There is a joy in sacrifice for others that is divine. *"My joy* I give unto you!" Joy on the eve of Calvary! This is the experiential path. Shall we follow it? You say, Yes? Then, let the Holy Spirit manage you, *and your circumstances*, and carry it out in His own way.

Let me, as I close, just give a word of personal experience. I was quite a babe in the consecrated life when God began to teach me these things. I remember once I was utterly sick with the joy of being used by Him to win one soul. The joy was so great that I said, "Oh Lord, I really cannot bear it!" He said so softly in reply, "How could you bear to be used to win five hundred?" And then He said, "Will you part with all that keen 'joy' which exhausts you, and just let Me have you and use you to others *with nothing for yourself?*" I saw the wisdom of this, and said, "Yes, Lord," and then found that I could go through marvelous scenes of blessing to others, which once would have quite overwhelmed me with "joy," without any exhaustion of my fragile frame! The secret of a fruitful life is, in brief, to pour out to others and *want nothing for yourself;* to leave yourself utterly in the hands of God, and not care what happens to you. I owe also a good deal to the books of Madame Guyon, and the way she showed the path to the life in God. The first time I read her life it deeply moved me. I was at the vicarage at Richmond (Surrey) in Mrs. Evan Hopkins' room. I was quite a young Christian. I had never heard of Madame Guyon, but in that room I picked up her Life, and asked if I might have it to read. I was just at the height of a glorious experience of the Baptism of the Holy Spirit. The glory of the Lord's conscious presence with me was so unspeakably sweet that it was most difficult to bring the mind to the ordinary affairs of life. But as I read the book, I clearly saw the way of the cross and all that it would mean. At first I flung the book away and said, "No! I will not go that path—I shall lose my 'glory' experience." But the next day I picked it up again, and the Lord whispered so gently, "If you want deep life and unbroken communion with God, this is the way." I thought, "Shall I? No!" And again I put the book away. The third day I again picked it up. Once more the Lord spoke: "If you want *fruit,* this is the path! I will not take the conscious joy-life from you; you may keep it if you like. But it is either that *for yourself,* or this *and fruit.* Which will you have?" And then, by His grace, I said "I choose the path of death for fruitfulness," and every bit of conscious experience closed. I walked for a time in such complete darkness— what Guyon describes as the "darkness" of faith—that it seemed as if God did not exist. Again by His grace I said, "Yes, I have only got what I agreed to," and on I went. I did not know what the outcome of this would be until I went to take some meetings, and then I saw the "fruit." It was just as if the people had been soaked in a life-tide from heaven! It was not a case of individual blessing—the people were all submerged in a floodtide of life from God which quickened them, released them, and brought them out into a new life. I did not need to speak personally to them. There seemed nothing to do but to give the message as God gave it to me, and the Holy Spirit did the rest. From that hour I understood, and knew intelligently, that it was "dying" and not "doing" that produced spiritual fruit. May God open our eyes to see the path, and to consent to follow Christ in His call to go with Him into the earth to die and thus bring forth fruit that shall remain for eternity.

5

THE LIFE-SIDE OF THE CROSS

"Raised with Him. . . ."
Colossians 2:12

D R. MABIE says in one of his books: "In the thought of Scripture the reconciling death, and resurrection, have always been taken together. They are inseparable parts of a real unity—TWIN PARTS OF ONE FACT." This is a very clear statement and true; but in experience, and in teaching also, the danger lies in not giving the "twin parts" equal balance. This affects the practical results in the life, for you cannot have the "positive" life-power without the negative death-application. If there is too much "negative," that is *death*—then there is too little "positive" in the practical life. Yet if you over-emphasize the "positive"—the "life" of the resurrection—then you do not get sufficient "negative" of the death-application to deal with the old Adam-life, which is in the way of the new creation and has to be dealt with by the "death" making room for the Christ-life. Therefore the two should have equal emphasis, and, so to speak, run together in the Christian life—death and life, Calvary and the resurrection—"twin parts of one fact."

Let me repeat again: In the experience of the believer, it is exactly in proportion to one's experiential apprehension, and of the co-working of the Spirit of God in applying the "negative" side of "death with Christ," that he gets the actual, experiential, and "positive" impartation of the power of the resurrection. *The two sides of these truths should evenly run together.* It is for lack of seeing this that there are so many one-sided Christians. They are either so "negative"— by dwelling much on the "death" side—that they have no activity of life, or they are so anxious to avoid the "negative"—the over-emphasis on "death"—that they dwell too much upon the "positive" side of life, and *in experience are in danger of calling the old life of nature the life of the resurrection.* We have need of the balance, so as to obtain a real impartation of the life of God. But it is so "human" to go to extremes! It is only as we know the danger, and rely upon God to guard us, that we can be kept spiritually sober, and balanced in truth. When we are conscious of the difficulties of it on account of our human limitations, we are less dogmatic in our statements to others about ourselves and our "views." We can always be sure of all that is plainly written in the Word of God, but not always so sure that we personally have full knowledge of the meaning of His Word.

Now let us turn again to Romans 6 and see in verses 10 and 11 how it gives not only what we may call the *death-side* of the cross, but the key to the *life-side* of our union with Christ in His resurrection. "*He died once, and once only, unto sin; but He lives [forever] unto God.* Likewise reckon ye also yourselves to be dead indeed unto sin, but living unto God IN CHRIST JESUS." In the three words "IN Christ Jesus" we have the key to the life of union with the risen Lord. We have died with Christ on the cross, so that we may "live unto God" in another sphere altogether, "IN Christ Jesus."

If you look at verse 13 it reads: "*Give your-selves to God, as being restored to life from the dead,* and your members to His service as instruments. . . ." Now what does it mean to be "in Christ Jesus" on the resurrection side of the cross? Turn to Romans 7:4: "You . . . were made dead to the Law, by [union with] the body of Christ; that you might be married to another, even to *Him who was raised* from the dead." In the margin of Scofield's Bible the word is "joined." "Dead" is the "negative" side of the truth of death; "joined" to the risen Lord is the "positive" side of the truth. Twin parts of one fact. Therefore there is no impartation of His Risen life *apart from Himself.* Moreover the "joining" is a joining of spirit. "He that is joined to the Lord is one spirit" (1 Corinthians 6:17)— not one soul. Therefore the "negative" side of death with Christ means practically a breaking away, or severing, or cutting away, of that which prevents the joining of your spirit to the risen Christ. The experiential outcome of the cross is really a releasing of the *spirit*. It was held, so to speak, in the grip of the soul and of the "flesh." It was so entangled in the life of nature that it could not be fully joined to Him who is a quickening Spirit. But how is the "cutting away" done? How does the Spirit of God apply the cross, and bring about the death-severance whereby the spirit is free to be joined to Christ?

This we find in Hebrews 4:12. *"The Word of God liveth and worketh, and is sharper than any two-edged sword,* piercing even to *the dividing asunder of soul and spirit. . . ."* Here we have a dividing and something that is immaterial and intangible. The "Word" therefore is a spiritual weapon, acting like a sword in the spiritual sphere—as a sword cuts in the material realm—and actually "dividing" immaterial things. That part of the Word that does this is the "word of the cross" (1 Corinthians 1:18, RV), dividing soul from spirit—first by giving the believer the distinctions between the two, and secondly, severing the two as the believer yields to the operation of the "word of the cross" telling of the death with Christ.

It also says that the "Word" discerns and reveals the thoughts, because "all things are naked and opened in the eyes of Him with whom we have to do" (Hebrews 4:13). Notice that it is the Lord Himself using the sword to cut away the old life—*Him*, with whom we have to do. He alone knows how to wield the "sword of the Spirit," which will "cut" like a knife, so that the spirit is severed or "disentangled," as an old writer says, "from the embrace of the soul"!

This is all psychologically and experientially true. In Dr. Andrew Murray's *Spirit of Christ*, he gives in the Appendix a very clear explanation of the dividing of soul and spirit which has to be done in the believer. He explains how man fell from the "spirit" dominating his whole being, into the soul, and then again how the soul sank down into the flesh, so that at last God said of man, "He has become flesh." He descended from spirit to soul, and from soul to "flesh." The spirit of man, says Dr. Murray, is that in us which is capable of knowing God—spirit-consciousness. The soul is the seat of *self*-consciousness, and the body the seat of *sense*-consciousness. An understanding of simple Bible psychology is necessary for any apprehension of the full life of victory through the atoning work of our Lord Jesus Christ. There is more to be dealt with in us than what we call "sin," and there is more than "sin" which prevents our full knowledge of God.

Now to know in real experience the life-side of the cross, we must know not only death to sin but the word of the cross severing between "soul" and "spirit," so that the spirit is liberated to be joined to the risen Lord. Then through the channel of your spirit, "joined to the Lord [as] one spirit," the quickening life of Him who is a quickening Spirit *comes into the "soul"* in resurrection power. For the "soul" is not destroyed, nor is the individuality of the believer destroyed. We do not become automatons, but the "soul"—

the personality—should be animated from the spirit, instead of from the lower realm of the life of nature. We may say the same words, perform the same acts, but with a different source of animating life at the back of them.

When the spirit is thus "one spirit" with the risen Lord, it is *via* the spirit, into the mind, that we experience the leadings of the Spirit and intimate knowledge of the personal Christ. It is *through our spirits joined to Him* by the Holy Spirit that we "know" Him personally—for the whole purpose of the truth is that we should KNOW HIM as well as the power of His resurrection.

Now turn to Colossians 2:6–7 for more light on the meaning of the words "in Christ Jesus." "As, therefore, you first received Christ Jesus the Lord, so walk in Him." When we first "received" Christ, by a simple act of faith, we were put *into Him* by the operation of the Spirit of God. Christ is in us, and our spirits are joined to Him as the Risen One, but we are also to abide "*in Him*" as a sphere in which we are to walk day by day. As we began, so we are to continue— simply trusting and relying upon Him, and abiding IN HIM. The *life*-side of the cross means to be "alive" to God—"*in Christ Jesus.*"

"Having in HIM your root," continues the apostle. You cannot be "rooted" in one place today and in another place the next. Therefore see to your roots. "*Having in Him your root.*" "Thou bearest not the root, but the root thee"! "And *in Him the foundation* whereon you are continually built up, persevering steadfastly in your faith. . . ." This clearly shows the need of our understanding the cross as the basic position from which we must never be moved. It is into His *death* that we are to be rooted. We cannot ever pass on into a life where we get past the cross, or advance to any goal, leaving the cross behind. To do so is like a tree refusing to root itself into the ground. We are to reckon ourselves "dead indeed unto sin" and living unto God, but it is "IN CHRIST JESUS." "In Him" we must be "rooted," and "in Him" have our "foundation," whereon we are continually to be built up; *i.e.,* we must ever be *striking our roots deeper into His death.*

Let us go back just here to John 3:16, and see how the being "in Christ Jesus" began at the initial stage of our new life. The words read, "God so loved the world that He gave His only begotten Son, that whosoever believeth *into Him*" should have life. Why the translators of the Bible into English have used the word "on" instead of "into," I do not know. We do not merely believe "on" Christ, but we believe *into* Him. Newberry says that the word "into" in the original has in it the thought of motion and thus is very suggestive; *i.e.,* as you "believe into" Christ, you are taken in by the co-action of the Holy Spirit. And *Calvary* is the place where this is done. The Lord Christ preached His own cross at the beginning of His ministry. He told Nicodemus of the necessity of the new birth and told him of His forthcoming death that sinners might have life. He said in John 3:14–15, "As Moses lifted up the serpent in the wilderness, even so must the Son of Man be lifted up: that whosoever believeth *into Him* should . . . have eternal life." We are put "into" Him in His death, and then "into" Him in His life, on the resurrection side of the cross, "having *in Him* your root"! Therefore "persevere steadfastly in your faith . . .": *i.e.*, when you first received Christ Jesus the Lord, you believed into Him; now stay in Him, be rooted in Him, have your foundation in Him, have all your spirit-life built up in Him.

Now turn to Colossians 2:9–11. "IN HIM dwells all the fullness"! It is as we abide in Him that we get the "fullness" of the Spirit. You say, "Oh, I want to be filled with the fullness of God!" Yes, but you can only hold, shall we say, a "teacup" full! Paul puts it quite another way—"*In Him* you have your fullness"! You have died with Him; now joined in spirit to Him, abide in Him and *you are in an ocean of life.* "*In Him* dwells all the fullness of the Godhead in bodily form, and *in Him you have your fullness;* for He is the Head of all Principalities and Powers. *In Him,* also, you were circumcised with a circumcision not made with hands, even the off-casting of the whole body of the flesh." The "flesh" cannot be taken "into Him." It must be "cast off." "For with Him you were buried in your baptism [into death], wherein also you were made partakers of His resurrection, through the faith wrought in you by God, who raised Him from the dead." Here again are the "twin parts of one fact."

The severing work of the cross takes place *as we abide in Him;* the cutting off of the "flesh," even the "off-casting of the whole body of the flesh," takes place *as we abide in Him.* It is a "circumcision" which is done without human hands, for it is wrought by the Holy Spirit as the believer consents, and trusts Him to carry out in him the full work of the cross of Christ. It is the Spirit of God who baptizes us into the death of Christ, and gives the believer the power to cast off all the "body of the flesh," and to carry this out in detail so that he may live according to God in the Spirit.

Now let us see two or three verses for the practical outworking in the life: "Whosoever, then, is *in Christ,* is a new creation; his old being has passed away, and behold, all has become new" (2 Corinthians 5:17). "*In Christ Jesus* neither circumcision is anything, nor uncircumcision, but a new creation" (Galatians 6:15). "In Christ" nothing is made to depend upon any external thing. "In Christ Jesus" nothing avails, nothing is of any use, nothing is of any account, except a new creation. Going into the sphere of Christ, we leave outside the "old." Abiding in Him, we may conform to the externalities of religious things—but you do not rely upon them, or place undue emphasis upon them, or ever allow them to become a cause of division between you and other children of God. Thus you will never find a child of God that you cannot get into spirit touch with, for you will always recognize that you have one life in the Lord.

Now turn to Ephesians 2:4–6. "God who is rich in mercy, because of the great love wherewith He loved us, even when we were dead in sin, called us to share the life of Christ. . . . And *in*

Christ Jesus, He raised us up with Him from the dead and seated us with Him in the heavens." In Christ is our root and our foundation, from which we must never move, but here we see the outcome of that death position. Joined to Him in spirit we are seated *with Him in spirit "in the heavens."* "Crucified with Him," we are called to share His life, "for ye are dead, and your life is hid with Christ in God" (Colossians 3:3). Resurrection power is *uplifting* power. Joined to the Risen One it can lift your spirit up, and keep it "far above all" in Christ, however deeply it may have been "down" under the bondage of the flesh, or mingled with the life of nature of the soul—for we are "seated with Him in the heavens" by union with Him who on His ascension "sat down." Joined to Him, He holds us as we abide and *rest* in Him.

Now finally as to the "life-side of the cross" in service. Let us turn to the sixth chapter of Ephesians, verse 10. It is to those who are "in Christ" as set forth in the early chapters of the Epistle that the apostle now opens up spiritual service and warfare. He begins this closing passage, this summing up of the life he had been describing, with the word "Finally." "Finally . . . let your hearts be strengthened in the Lord, and in the conquering power of His might. . . ." The Lord Christ, Paul said in chapter one, is *above* the Principalities and the Powers. He is not under them, and the believer is also seated with Him "far above." Now, let such a one be *strengthened* in the Lord, be confident, be sure, know for certain the position of victory, and be strong in the conquering power of His might.

Also, in this place of assured victory, "Put on the whole armor of God" (verse 11). You know your position, now be established there, and put on the armor of God, "that you may be able to *stand.*" But you were "seated" a moment ago! Yes, you cannot "fight" external foes if you have a conflict within! You must be "sitting down" inside! If you lose your inward peace you are at the mercy of the devil. For conquering warfare the believer must have the inward calm of God, and be strengthened, stablished, rooted in Him. Now "put on the armor" that you may be able to stand.

And why need we "stand"? Because of "*the wiles of the devil.*" This is all his scheming, strategy, methods, planned to get you out of your victorious position. The wiles that you do not see are the most dangerous. They are planned against you from morning to night. You say that you do not want to be thinking about "evil spirits" all the time? *But they will be thinking of you.* You are only called to think about them to the end that you may be on the alert in perpetual prayer. The knowledge that they are perpetually planning to ensnare you drives you nearer to God in prayer that their wiles do not succeed. As you do this your eyes will be opened to *see* their wiles, and you will keep steady and quiet when you discern them at work upsetting things in your home, to draw you out of your place in God.

"*Stand firm against the wiles of the devil, for the adversaries with whom we wrestle are not flesh and blood.*" It is strange, in the face of this, how God's people perpetually see only "flesh and blood" as the cause of the conflict and trouble in their lives. They will not recognize that there are spiritual foes. Or if at the back of circumstantial troubles they see some other cause than the flesh and blood, they put all down to the "will of God." By some means or other, they will ignore the supernatural powers of evil. In the one case they have friction with the ones who injure them, and in the latter they submit, as they think, to the "will of God," and become actual victims of the forces of Satan attacking and seeking to injure every child of God. They do not know how to discern between what is really of God and what is of Satan. The apostle says *our real adversaries are not flesh and blood*. These spiritual foes are in the aerial heavens. They roam in the air around our planet, seeking to do all the evil that they can. It is very manifest just now in Britain—not to speak of other lands. These powers are working upon the people in an intensified form, and arousing the fallen Adam in them. The wave of Spiritism has much to do with it. It is not possible to have thousands of people communicating with demons, under the deception of speaking with their dead relatives, without these demons influencing the atmosphere of the whole country.

Our adversaries are not flesh and blood, but they are Princes—"the Principalities, and the Powers, and the Sovereigns of this present darkness." We have three hierarchic ranks of Satan's governmental powers described here. The "Princes" set over "Principalities"; the "Powers"—

those who are able to use the resources of the air; and the "Sovereigns"—the kings or rulers, governing "this present darkness." Then last and lowest in rank are the multitudes of "spirits of evil in the heavens" who carry out the behests of Satan their chief and the other "rulers" of their various spheres.

In Daniel 10 the veil is lifted, and we are told about a "Prince of *Persia*" and a "Prince of *Grecia*" (Daniel 10:13, 20), withstanding the heavenly messengers to Daniel. Is there not a "Prince of *England*" and a "Prince of *France*"? In every land do not God's people wrestle against the "Princes" of the satanic forces?

Then what about the "Powers" wielding for Satan the forces of the air? What resources they have to carry out their plans! We are only in this century learning about wireless telegraphy, and electricity, but the satanic "Prince of this World" knew about them—and other "powers" yet unknown to us—centuries ago. This is why "lies" spread like poison gas, and "truth" has to fight its way. This is why the spirit of lawlessness is able to spread far and wide so quickly, and to lay hold of men and inspire them with delusions which, if allowed their way, will wreck others and themselves. There are "waves" of satanic delusions sent forth by the "Powers" in the invisible realm, like a wave of electric currents, invisibly spreading, and drawing people under its power.

Then there are the "Sovereigns" of the "darkness." The Princes lead the fight like generals (Daniel 10:13), the "Powers" wield the forces of the air, but the "Kings" or rulers govern the *darkness.* Their work is to plan how to keep people in the dark; to prevent truth and light from reaching them—in brief, not only to frustrate the gospel but to hinder truth and all light that comes from truth, in every way they can. The "spirits of evil" are the multitudinous hosts of demons swarming about and carrying out personal attacks on individuals for the fulfilling of the world plans of their Prince.

The standing against the wiles of these, as described in Ephesians 6:11, *is the prelude to the aggressive war against them.* The believer "strong in the Lord," on the defensive against the wiles, is called to the aggressive; and by the wielding of the weapon of Christ's victory over them at Calvary, these foes can all be dislodged and driven from their strongholds. Yes, the plans of their chiefs can be frustrated and broken up. The apostle says this plainly, and tells us how. "Wherefore," he writes, "take up with you to the battle the whole armor of God, that you may be able to *withstand* [Gr. resist] them in the evil day, and HAVING OVERTHROWN THEM ALL, TO STAND UNSHAKEN." This clearly depicts an aggressive advance, with the sure and certain fact that they can be "overthrown," yes, by the Lord's children in union with Him. There are "evil days," when the "princes" and "powers" and the "rulers of the darkness" come and besiege, say for instance, your church. Do not only stand on the defensive and protect yourself, but looking not at "flesh and blood" *go up to that battle* with the hosts of darkness, strong in the Lord—anchored in Him, with the eternal calm of God centered in your being—and "overthrow" the invisible hosts by the weapon of faith and prayer. Remember God is on the Throne, and when you are centered there in Him, you partake of His strength, "rooted and fixed in God." Strong "in the Lord," you can safely take the initiative against principalities and powers and go up to the battle with confidence, because your "defensive" is sure.

"*Having overthrown them all,*" writes the apostle, you can then "stand unshaken." So there is a "battle"—a specific onslaught upon you, or upon the church, described as "the evil day"— and there is an "overthrow" of that specific attack of the enemy, and then a standing back in God in blessed victory. All this is part of the believer's experience on the "life-side of the cross." He is not only "joined to the Lord, one Spirit" for sharing in His resurrection life, and for victory over sin and the "flesh," but he is joined to Him to be sent forth by Him to "overthrow" the forces of darkness seeking to "overthrow" the church of God, and to frustrate or delay the Lord's appearing. The great need of today is that the Lord's children should apprehend the call to battle, and rise up in His strength to face the foe. It is not enough to simply "endure"—crying out "Oh Lord, how long?" The Lord must have those who work with Him to "overthrow" in glorious victory all the hosts of Satan, hindering his plans, until as victors they are caught away to meet the Lord. *Twos and threes meeting together in prayer can become strategic centers for the overthrow of Satan's onslaughts on the people and the work of God.* If they only know how to "pray" against the foe! If they only know how to take their stand in God, and wield the weapon of Calvary's victory!

6

THE CROSS AND LIFE IN THE SPIRIT

"We have died . . . new service of the Spirit"
Romans 7:6

THIS morning when speaking of the life-side of the cross, we were more occupied with the word "life" than the word "spirit." On the life- or resurrection-side of the cross, we have seen there is the joining of the spirit to the Spirit of Christ, for "he that is joined to the Lord is one spirit." In the early days of my Christian life I thought that everything that took place in my spirit was the action of the Holy Spirit, not understanding clearly all that the Bible says about the human spirit. Let us trace it out.

1. *There is a human spirit.* 1 Corinthians 2:11 shows this clearly. "Who can know what belongs to man, but the spirit of man which is within him?" *i.e.,* who can know what is going on within us but the *spirit* which is within us?

"Even so," says the apostle, "none can know what belongs to God, but the Spirit of God alone." Even as others can only know our inmost thoughts as we choose to reveal them, so we can only know God as His Spirit reveals Him. "Now we have received, not the spirit of the world, but the Spirit which is of God, that we might *understand* those things which have been freely given us by God." We see by this passage that there is a "spirit of man" which knows the man, as the "Spirit of God" knows the "depths of God." Also that God gives to men who will receive Him, His Spirit, so that by His Spirit they may be enabled to understand the things of God—things which they could not know apart from the teaching of His Spirit.

2. *The spirit of man is a distinct entity or organism* (1 Corinthians 5:4). "You convene an assembly, and when you, and *my spirit* with you, are gathered together. . . ." Here is Paul talking about his own spirit being present with the assembled believers in Corinth. Here we have the fact of there being a spirit of man as a distinct entity, or organism. Again in 1 Corinthians 14:14, Paul says, "If I utter prayers in a tongue, *my spirit* indeed prays, but my *understanding* bears no fruit." So "spirit" and mind, or understanding, are not the same thing! "My spirit prays," says the apostle, apart entirely from the "soul"—or understanding. This shows that there is prayer which takes place only in the spirit, without the "understanding" of what the prayer is about (see Romans 8:26), and without expression by the voice, or "feelings" of the body. So, the

apostle says, "I will pray indeed with my spirit, but I will pray with my understanding also; I will sing praises with *my spirit*, but I will sing with my understanding also." This prayer in the *spirit* is not of value to others gathered in a meeting. "For if thou, *with thy spirit*, offerest praise" only, "how shall the Amen be said" by others who are present? The "understanding" prayer is needed in the assembly.

3. *The varied characteristics of the spirit.* Now look at the varied expressions which are used concerning the spirit. These characteristics may belong to the spirit of man itself, or be brought about in it by the action of the Holy Spirit. Romans 12:11 speaks of a "fervent" spirit, something quite different from "enthusiasm" or fervor in the *soul.* The "fervent" *spirit* is the same in a revival meeting and in the cold drudgery of daily life. It is this fervency that the world misses in the children of God. People have the counterfeit of it in the things of the world, stirred by the life of nature; surely the children of God should have it from the source of the Spirit of God, setting their spirits on fire. Then it would come out in every detail of life—in action and service, even in handshaking— which can be the warm, heartening expression of a fervent spirit. We are needing sorely, in a selfish world, an intensity which comes from a true fervency of *spirit.*

In 2 Corinthians 7:13, Paul says that the "spirit" of Titus had been "refreshed" by seeing the zeal (fervency) of the Corinthian believers in the things of God. Some of you are getting your spirits "refreshed" here! Again in Acts 18:5, we read that Paul was "pressed in spirit" to "testify to the Jews that Jesus was Christ." This shows the action of the Holy Spirit in the man's spirit urging him to a certain course of action. It is when testimony, or preaching, has its source in this pressure of the *spirit*—not merely the impulse or emotion of the soul—that there are eternal results in blessing to those who are prepared by the Holy Spirit to respond to it. Sometimes the pressure in the spirit is so strong that the man can hardly breathe until the "testimony" is given. Those who know the active in-working of the Holy Ghost learn to recognize His working in them in this way, and how to discern all that is spurious, or arises from the counterfeit produced by Satan as an "angel of light."

In reference to this we have in Acts 20:22–23 a remarkable passage, showing the way Paul was able to read the mind of the Holy Spirit, as made known in his own spirit. He said to the elders at Miletus: "As for me, behold I go to Jerusalem *in spirit* foredoomed to chains, . . . in every city the Holy Spirit gives the same testimony that bonds and afflictions await me." In his own spirit Paul knew that he was going forward into "bonds," and knew this to be the testimony of the Holy Spirit in his spirit. Here is seen clearly the co-action of the Holy Spirit with the human spirit—the spirit of man as the organ, and the Spirit of God working in and through it. This pure spirit working is distinct from the soul (natural), or the life after the flesh, *i.e.*, the emotional aspect of the soul, or the "feelings" of the body.

In Romans 1:9, again we read: "Whom I serve with the worship of *my spirit.*" The apostle knew the life of the spirit, not only as the organ through which the Holy Spirit moved him in prayer, in fervency, in testimony, but also in service to his Lord. This does not mean that the spirit is not under the man's control. That it always is so is seen in 1 Corinthians 14:32, where Paul says that the gift of prophecy does not take from the prophets the control of their own spirits. They have not control over the Holy Spirit, of course, but the man has control over his own spirit in its co-action with the Spirit of God, for the Holy Spirit does not deprive the redeemed soul of his freedom of action and decision of will to voluntarily work with God.

4. *The work to be done in the spirit of man.* In Romans 7:6, the apostle speaks about "*newness of spirit.*" "A new spirit will I put within you" was the promise of God to Israel, made through Ezekiel, long before the time of Paul. The new birth therefore, or regeneration, takes place in the spirit. The spirit of man by nature is a fallen spirit. It is "spirit," but it is separate from God—in darkness and emptiness. It is consequently open to the spirits of Satan, and able to give place to evil spirits and become their medium of communication with others. But in the new birth the spirit is brought back to God by regeneration, and man is given again power to know God.

In 2 Corinthians 7:1, we read: "Having these

promises (*i.e.*, the indwelling of God, ch. 6:16–18)
. . . let us cleanse ourselves from every defilement,
either of flesh *or spirit.*" Here we see that the
"spirit" can be defiled. There are sins of the *spirit.*
For the indwelling of God it is necessary to
have a spirit without guile. "Blessed is the man
in whose spirit there is no guile . . . ," no
duplicity, no mixture. This is enough to show that
the spirit needs cleansing. And the believer is
to do this by acknowledging these sins, applying
to God to have them dealt with by the cross,
and by putting them away. We are to "cleanse
ourselves" not only from the defilement of the
flesh, but of the spirit. What may we describe as
sins of the spirit? Take, for example, a *jealous*
spirit, an *unkind* spirit, a *crooked* spirit. You
may trace all these in the Bible. In the Psalms
and Proverbs you will find all kinds of things
said about the spirit. And alas, when there are
sins of the spirit, they invite the evil spirits to
become attached to the man's spirit! For example:
when a man has a jealous spirit, an evil spirit
of jealousy takes hold of him and dominates
him, so that he loses all control of himself. The
most mischievous things of life are those that
come from the spirit. We prove this perpetually
in daily life. You say: If the man's *spirit* is all
right we can get along! And it is so. Mistakes
and blunders of judgment and action can all be
put right, but when the *spirit* is wrong—all is
wrong. "Lord, cleanse my heart," you say. But
we consist of more than "hearts." The heart is
the seat of the affections. It is true that out of
the heart are the issues of life, and the heart is

described as the "reins" of man, for he is governed by his affections. But the heart may be right and the "*spirit*" still needs cleansing from, for example, "guile"! How few are "without guile," *i.e.,* without mixture—without "suspicion" of others—without duplicity, saying something they do not mean, pretending something they do not feel. There are people with a suspicious spirit, always watching for and expecting something wrong. They cannot believe anything good. They have not a spirit "without guile"! How beautiful it is not to be looking for evil, and to take what others say with purity of spirit! Not thinking always that others have ulterior motives. How quickly conscious a sensitive spirit is of this spirit among God's people. Oh, that we may put away this thing and have a spirit "without guile."

In the light of this you will now see why the spirit needs to be divided from the soul. This must be emphasized again here. "The Word of God is quick and powerful . . . *piercing even to the dividing asunder of soul and spirit.*" This is the deepest work to be done by the Word of God for the renewal of the believer through the redemption that is in Christ Jesus. We have already seen that before the Fall, as God created man, the *spirit* was the dominant power, ruling the soul— the personality of the man—for the expression of the life of God, with the body as the slave. Then we see how man fell—so that the flesh ruled instead of the spirit (Genesis 6:3, 6). Then how the Son of God came, and as the Representative Man took the fallen Adam to the cross, where in its stead He suffered the penalty of death for sin, and in Him the fallen Adam died. "If One died for all—then all died" (2 Corinthians 5:14). Now the work of the Spirit through the Word of God is to apply the Lord Christ's finished work on the cross to every man and reverse the results of the Fall. The spirit of man, joined to the risen Lord, is to be again the ruling power, governing the "soul," controlling the mind, the emotions and dispositions—and then the body the obedient vehicle (Romans 6:13) at the command of God through the "new creation." This is the meaning of the cross. The precious blood cleanses the heart, the affections, but *the cross deals with the old creation.*

Someone asks me, Is there not a difference between the "flesh" and the "old man"? The Word of God throws light on this. In some passages we find Paul speaking of the "flesh" as purely "flesh and blood." "Though living in the flesh, my warfare is not waged according to the flesh" (2 Corinthians 10:3), he writes. So in this sense we are "in the flesh" even when the "old man" is crucified. But the apostle adds that even though we are thus "living in the flesh," we are *not to act* "*according to the flesh,*" but "according to God in the spirit." "Living in the flesh," in a right sense, is not to be an excuse for yielding to it, or being governed by it in any degree.

Now let us look at 1 Thessalonians 5:23, giving a summary of the work to be done in the believer as the outcome of the finished work of Christ on the cross. "May the God of Peace Himself sanctify you wholly; and may your spirit and soul and body all together be preserved blameless, at the appearing of our Lord Jesus Christ." Note the order: *spirit* first, then soul, then body. Note the word "sanctify"—*set you apart* altogether for God, and keep you blameless.

5. *The working of the Holy Spirit in the spirit of a man.* Romans 8:16 very clearly shows this aspect of the spiritual life: "The Spirit bears witness with *our own spirit* that we are the children of God." This is not the "understanding" or the mind. The Holy Spirit gives His witness *in our spirits.* Look at Ephesians 3:16: "He would grant you strength by the entrance of His Spirit into your inner man." This is, says Moule, "Deep in it, penetrating far into it, *the regenerate human spirit. . . .*" Here is the truth made clear. The Holy Spirit dwells and works in the human spirit. It is His shrine, and His place of abode. He desires to penetrate far into it, so as to produce, shall I say, the *fusion* of the regenerate human spirit with the Spirit of Christ, for the sole object of the working of the Spirit of God in us is to unite us to Christ and bring about in us conformity to His likeness.

6. *A Bible picture of a "spiritual man."* For this we turn again to 1 Corinthians 2:11. The "spiritual" man has an acute "spirit" sense. He *knows* the action of his spirit, and by his spirit knows all about himself. It is only when a man becomes really "spiritual," with the soul divided from his spirit (*i.e.,* the mixture of mental and spiritual separated), that this is realized. The majority of people are in a "fantasy," as an old writer says, about themselves. The mental perception is unable to penetrate into the depths

of "yourself" and make you know yourself as you really are. The man's own spirit, unmixed with the intellect, "knows" himself, and he receives the Holy Spirit into his spirit that he may know God (verse 12).

Then the spiritual man, with the Holy Spirit dwelling in his spirit, is given a spirit-faculty which enables him to *understand* the things of God, and to explain them to others. "These are things whereof we speak, in words not taught by man's wisdom, but by the Spirit, *explaining* spiritual things to spiritual men." The Revised Version says "*comparing* spiritual things with spiritual," and the RV margin "*combining*," and "*interpreting*." Conybeare says "explaining," and in the RV margin of verse 15 we have the word "*examining*"—the Greek meaning being "to investigate and decide." Now if we put all these renderings together, you have a striking description of the spiritual man in his dealing with the "things of God"—showing, too, that God desires us not only to trust Him, but to *understand Him,* and that the Holy Spirit is given to us with this object. Practically it means that when the man's spirit is actually "joined" with the risen Lord, the Holy Spirit gives him a spirit sense, or faculty, whereby he is able to "compare" or "examine" spiritual things, and "combine" spiritual facts with spiritual. As the chemist in his laboratory compares, combines, examines, searches, so the spiritual man deals with spiritual things, combining, comparing, explaining, interpreting, examining; *e.g.,* he "investigates" the spiritual causes of spiritual phenomena until he is able to "decide" their source! But where are the spiritual men, able to do this in this perilous time? Ability to deal with the "letter" of the Scriptures there may be, but alas, alas, how few can handle the "things of the spirit" so as to be able to interpret these "things" to others.

I have been feeling lately the responsibility of those who know the Scriptures in the original Greek. Most of the errors among God's children come from a misuse of faulty translations of the original. Yet with all the aids to non-Greek readers available today, people do not take trouble to search, examine, and *investigate* what the God-breathed Word says in the language used by the Holy Ghost. Oh that men who know the original Scriptures took trouble to explain the things of God to those who do not know the Greek language. There are deep wells of life from God, and fathomless depths of the deep things of God, hidden away in "roots" of the Greek original Scriptures. Undoubtedly God chose that language as the one in which He could best make known spiritual things to His redeemed ones. But let us be of good courage. The Holy Spirit can teach us. I was once in a company of Convention speakers, when they asked me about some passage in the Word, and I said, "I do not know Greek, *but the Holy Ghost does!*" I have been amazed to find that when spiritual things have been opened to me truly by Him, they have always proved to be in harmony with the Greek original. This gave me confidence, and greater reliance upon the Holy Spirit to open to me the true meaning of the Word. It also made me careful not to say a certain verse meant this or that until I was given His light upon it. Then when He truly gave the light, I have never found that those who knew the Greek could contradict what *the Holy Ghost had opened.* It made me careful also to search the Word of God, and to use every possible help for the understanding of the original. There are many such "helps" today. If we honestly want to know what God says and are willing to be delivered from human "views" of the Word, He will teach us.

The primary condition on our part is to have the work of the cross wrought in us, even to "the dividing of soul and spirit," so that we may have an acute spirit-sense, for you can *"sense" the meaning of some deep things of God* which you cannot grasp with your intellect. Some call this "intuition," but it is more than that, for the intuition of the unregenerate does not open to them the things of God. The "intuition" of the spiritual man comes from the human spirit indwelt by the Holy Spirit. It appears then that the "mind" and spirit become one, or else it is that the Holy Spirit penetrates the mind, clarifying and illuminating it, so that it loses its earth-born character. Possibly this is what the apostle meant when he said, "Be renewed in the *spirit* of your mind." The intellect then becomes spiritual. For it is with the mind that we perceive, and with the spirit that we "know," or "feel" or *sense* the things of God. Paul is an example of this. He had one of the most brilliant intellects of his age, and of all later ages. But in the things of God, his intellect had been renewed and inter-penetrated by the Holy Spirit until he "combined," "compared" and "interpreted" the things of God, unknown, and unreachable, by the unregenerate man.

When truth thus comes to the teacher who is taught of God, it is *borne witness to in the consciences of those to whom you speak.* It need not be forced upon anyone by the speaker, for the Holy Ghost does His own work and bears witness to His own Word.

7. *The laws of the spirit; and how to walk after the Spirit.*

(a) First there is the minding of the things of the spirit. See Romans 8:5–6: "They who live after the flesh *mind fleshly things,* but they who live after spirit"—the article is not there in the original—"*mind spiritual things;* and the fleshly mind is death; but the spiritual mind is life and peace." The secret of walking after the Spirit is, briefly, to "mind" the spirit, and put spiritual things first. As we do this, it means that you never lose consciousness of what is going on in your spirit. Madame Guyon has a helpful illustration of what it means to abide in Christ. She says that when you enter a room you may sense how pleasant and warm it is, but as you stay in it you have no "consciousness" save of ease. But go into the cold outside and you will soon know that you are not "abiding" in the room. Walking in the Spirit, and minding the spirit, therefore, does not always mean any consciousness in the senses, but a keen intuitive knowledge of God and His will. It is not a life of great spirit phenomena but of quiet rest in God in the common things of daily life. The believer thus "minding the spirit" ceases to be governed by "circumstances" and to measure external acts by their external values. Your great and blessed rest lies in simply and quietly doing the will of God, for in the life of union with God the person cheerfully, gladly, does the common everyday things with the same fervency of spirit as he would do what is called "the Lord's work."

(b) Then there is the being *obedient to the monitions of the Spirit.* "All who are led by God's Spirit, and they alone, are the sons of God" (Romans 8:14). The Spirit of God *leads* those who are truly sons of God—begotten in the Divine Nature—by various workings in the human spirit, such as impressions, drawings, restrainings, assurance in prayer, and inward witness to an action being in the will of God. All these monitions of the Holy Spirit in the spirit of the believer are very delicate and subtle, but they can be known and read as the life in the spirit becomes stronger and less mixed with the emotions and impulses of the soul or the activities of the mind. This subject in all its ramifications would take too much time to deal with now, but as one example, suppose you are asked to do a certain thing, but you find that in your spirit there is a sense of deadness toward that course. It is then always safe to wait and pray for more light. The inner "restraint" generally means God's "No." You go into a meeting where strange and abnormal manifestations are taking place. In your *spirit* there is a shrinking and a repugnance. It is never safe to go against this, and always safe not to force yourself to accept supernatural things. "As many as are *led . . .*" writes the apostle. The Spirit of God does not force, but leads the obedient child of God—so gently that only when he is quiet and still he is conscious of it. Another very important point in obeying the monitions of the Holy Spirit is not to act in anything without *deliberate volition.* If there is in your spirit any "impression" or "drawing" to this or that, it must never be followed without your having examined it in the light of the Word of God and come to a deliberate, intelligent decision that it is of God.

(c) There is also a need of *knowledge of God, and His ways of working.* In Philippians 1:9 we read, "This I pray, that your love may abound yet more and more in true knowledge, and in all *understanding, teaching you to distinguish good from evil.*" The Holy Spirit can give us this "understanding" so that we may be able to distinguish good from evil in our path. Colossians 1:9–11 again speaks of this as a necessity for walking worthy of God.

(d) A very important law of the spirit-life is that of "expression." This we find in John 7:38. "He that *believeth into* Me . . . *out of* his belly shall flow rivers of living water. This spake He of the Spirit. . . ." Briefly, if there is an influx, *there must be an "outflow."* Many of the Lord's children are suffering from "suppressed spirit." Just as you would suffer if you had no physical exercise, so the spirit suffers if it has no "outflow" or "exercise." The spirit-life in us must have expression, or it becomes passive and feeble. When it is in normal activity the life in it "overflows" easily—quite a different thing to the talkativeness of the life of nature. We get a gleam into this in what is said of Peter in Acts 4:8: "Then Peter, filled with the Holy Ghost, said unto them. . . ." There was a fresh influx of the Spirit of God into his spirit, and out in bold testimony. "Out" of you "shall flow rivers of living water." We shall never have a fuller spiritual life than the extent to which we *pour out* that life to others. This hindering "reserve" which is locking up the spirit in so many needs breaking down. It produces a conflict in service for God which you need not have. Ask therefore for the fullness of the Spirit in your spirit, and then "give," and it shall again be given unto you.

(e) Lastly there is *the use of the spirit in spiritual conflict.* We have already dealt with this as part of the life on the resurrection side of the cross. The Holy Spirit will teach us the true use of the spirit in conflict, for He alone can show us how to distinguish the things that differ, in the spiritual realm. I will only say that the use of the *spirit only* makes the believer very quiet in conflict. The victory is often won by a quiet and simple word. It is the *Holy Spirit who makes the spirit strong to stand against opposing powers.*

7

THE CROSS AND POWER FOR SERVICE

THERE are so many lines of teaching on the enduement of power for service that numbers of the Lord's children are perplexed, and in some cases hindered from receiving what they need to equip them for effective witnessing about Christ. The trouble lies in the fact that in this, as in many other aspects of truth, *the cross has not been given its right place* as the central point from which the Holy Spirit works.

The consequence is that one-sided truth is given on the subject, colored generally by the experience of the teacher. The grace and patience of God, however, is seen in the way that He bears witness to all that is "truth," in any degree, even when it is given without due regard to other aspects of it.

Let us take the Word, and with the cross as the "fixed point" from which we are seeking to view every subject, see what light we can get in the matter.

First let me say definitely that *there is an "enduement of power" for service,* which every believer should know for effectiveness in life and service. If we look back into the history of those who have been greatly used by God—Moody, Finney and others—you will find that there was a moment in their lives when God dealt with them and gave them an enduement of power.

Then let us look broadly at the fact of "Pentecost" from the historical viewpoint. Historically there is only one "Calvary," one "Resurrection Day," one "Pentecost": *i.e.,* Calvary, where Christ died on the cross; the Resurrection, when He arose from the dead; Pentecost, when the Holy Ghost came into the Church.

Calvary is not to be repeated, nor the Resurrection, nor Pentecost in its historical meaning. The finished work of Christ on the cross, His glorious resurrection as the witness of the Father to the completeness of His finished work—these had their outcome in the outpoured Spirit at Pentecost. All was final, and pivotal in completeness as carried out by the Son of God through the Eternal Spirit.

But now in the experience of the Church, each one who becomes a member of that Church (*i.e.,* the *mystical organism* of the Body of Christ), puts in his claim to (1) all that *Calvary* means for him, (2) all that the *Resurrection* means for him, and, logically, (3) all that *Pentecost* means for him.

Now carry the analogy further: in appropriating our part in all that "Calvary" means, we do not expect the external historical facts to be repeated in us. We put in our claim for all that it means to have our sins borne by Christ, and to be crucified with Christ, but we do not expect an external "cross" with all the accompanying tragic events of Golgotha. Nor do we expect a visible corporeal "resurrection" exactly like the Lord coming out of the tomb—although we shall have a resurrection of the body by and by. Why then expect all the *historical externalities of Pentecost* to take place in us? Is not the present dispensation of the Spirit a *spiritual* one, during which God is calling out a people for His Name and building a *spiritual* temple as far in advance of the visible Temple as the sun above the moon?

What then is the *spiritual* and *inside* meaning of Calvary, the Resurrection and Pentecost, as they are to be known by the Church of God? If we are not to have the "externalities" of these wondrous events carried out in us, where shall we learn their inner application to us?

First as explained by the Lord Himself *before His death,* and second as explained by the Lord Himself *after His death,* when, as the Risen and Ascended Conqueror, He chose an instrument on earth through whom He could reveal the spiritual meaning of the historical facts of His death, resurrection and ascension. It is in the Epistles of Paul that we get the inside meaning of it all. For the glorified Lord chose the Apostle Paul to be the revelator to the Church, as Moses was God's revelator to Israel. He was chosen to give out to the world *Christ's* explanation of Calvary, and *Christ's* explanation of the Resurrection, and *Christ's* explanation of Pentecost, as He foreshadowed it in germ before He died. Therefore all that Calvary is for us, all that the Resurrection means to us, and all that Pentecost means to us, is to be learned in the Epistles of Paul, and not so much from the historical records of the Acts of the Apostles.

Let me emphasize here the importance of our remembering, when we read Paul's Epistles, *that all his teachings were directly given him by the ascended Christ.* Say to yourself as you read, This is not Paul's idea of Calvary and the blood, but the glorified Christ in heaven explaining His own cross, explaining His own resurrection, and what it meant to the Church—and also explaining the coming of the Holy Spirit, and His work in the believer, and in the Church.

We must therefore go to the Epistles to learn the true inside meaning of the enduement of power, and as we do so, remember to keep always together the triple group of (1) the Cross, (2) the Resurrection, and (3) Pentecost, for the obtaining of the full power of either. Also let us remember the sequence of God's dealing with us is in this order. Let us pray for the *deepest work of the cross* to be applied to us, the *fullest power of the resurrection,* and the *mightiest enduement of the Holy Spirit for service,* that it is possible for us to know.

It is because believers seek for their share of "Pentecost" without the deep bedrock work of the cross and the resurrection first to be wrought in them, that the devil as an angel of light has broken in upon believers with his counterfeits.

If the cross had been preached and known in all its aspects, the devil would not have been able to deceive, as he is doing, so many children of God. But the majority of Christians look upon the cross only as a place for the forgiveness of sins, where they get right with God. Then they cry for a "Pentecostal" enduement, without first asking for a *deep work of the Spirit—in the old Adam-life being nailed to the cross and rendered inoperative.* This is the only safe basic position for asking for an enduement of power. In the face of the spiritual perils of today through the outbreak of spiritism, it might mean disaster to many if we were given a floodtide of the Holy Ghost in revival power when the bedrock meaning of Calvary is so little known. This may be the reason it is withheld by our Father in heaven.

Now let us look at the Lord's explanation of Pentecost, before He died. This we find summarized in a few phrases in John 14:20. "AT THAT DAY YE SHALL KNOW THAT I AM IN MY FATHER, AND YE IN ME." "*That day,*" the context tells us, was the Day of Pentecost. His disciples listening to these words had walked the earth with Christ, and had seen Him and known Him as a man; after His resurrection they would see Him again as a man, but with a resurrection body. They were to handle Him and see for themselves that He had "flesh and bones" as a man, proving a real physical resurrection. They were to see this man ascend before their eyes into the heavens, while they were left on earth. But a "Day" would come when they would know the inside spiritual meaning of it all. At His ascension they knew that He had gone up to God. But there was more. "At that day ye shall know that I am in My Father, and *ye in Me*." The Holy Spirit would reveal to them that *they were in God also*—that the ascended Lord had taken them with Him in spirit back to God. "Christ died, the Just for the unjust, that He might bring us to God." Not only reconcile us to God, but in spirit reunite us *with* God. The severance caused by the Fall is removed. Through the cross the fallen Adam is crucified, "For *ye died*, and your life is hid *with Christ in God*." When "that Day" came, by the Holy Ghost they would know their source of life to be changed. They would understand they had died with Christ, and were translated out of the power of darkness into the kingdom of His dear Son.

We therefore gather from the Lord's words that the great inner meaning of Pentecost is the Holy Spirit making real to you your union with the ascended Christ. This is in harmony with the order we have already seen—Calvary, Resurrection, Pentecost. You first know your union with the crucified Christ, then your union with the risen Christ, and then your union with the ascended Lord in the bosom of the Father, which according to John 14:20 is "Pentecost." When the Holy Spirit came, the 120 knew experientially what Calvary, Resurrection and Pentecost meant. They knew they had died with their Lord, they knew they were joined to Him, and taken with Him unto God. Their entire outlook was changed in the upper room. From the moment the Holy Spirit came they looked out at the world *from the throne of God.* They understood the Lord's words, "As My Father hath sent Me, *even so send I you*" (John 20:21). They had been taken "back to God," and were now "sent" from God to proclaim His message to the world.

This is, practically, the "enduement of power" as foreshadowed by the Lord. It really means that by the influx of the Holy Spirit into your spirit, it has found its center. You are no longer "self-centered," but God-centered. It is when we are thus taken back, in union with the ascended Lord, to God the Father, that the Spirit of God is able to work out through us all that He wants to do. It is then that it may be said of you, as of Gideon, "The Spirit of the Lord clothed Himself with Gideon, and Gideon blew a trumpet!" It means not only the Holy Spirit in the believer, but the believer IN GOD, and therefore covered or clothed by Him. This is what is promised in Luke 24:49. The disciples were told to wait until the Holy Spirit had come, when they would be "clothed" with power from on high—power which would make them know they were with Christ in God.

Also the Lord said, *"and I in you."* The last is the result of the first condition. (1) "I am in My Father," (2) "ye are in Me," and (3) "I in you." This means dynamic power. What use to talk of having received a "power" that accomplishes nothing? "Power"—real power—is known by its *effects* and not by its noise! When the believer is deeply anchored in his divine center, "with Christ in God" he moves in an orbit of His will all the day long, as the planets move in their orbit in the heavens. Nothing is lost, or *ineffective*, when God is the moving force of your life, as you abide in Him. Centered in God the believer does not have to strain or struggle, but abiding in God he simply moves on with Him, accomplishing hour by hour, and day by day, the carrying out of God's plan for his life. When he is bidden to do "big things," he is not conscious that it is he who does them. There is no sense of "burden" under the heaviest burdens. *He moves with God,* and when he is bidden to act, he acts also with God, for God moves in and with him; therefore God is responsible, for He carries the burden, as the believer carries out His will.

"I IN YOU" is the outcome of thus being centered with Christ in God. When this is realized, there is relief from self-consciousness. The Holy Spirit clothing the believer makes the indwelling of Christ so real that he forgets himself and how he acts. He is moving in an eternal element, not only within but *around him,* which makes him "at home" everywhere. Thus he, so to speak, carries his own atmosphere with him. This is what David realized when he said, "If I make my bed in hell, behold, Thou art there!" Even in the midst of those opposed to Christ, we carry our own atmosphere with us. What a contrast between this life in God, with its ease and "naturalness," and the "mechanical" kind of life many Christians are trying to live. They have such a "process" for keeping it up, and maintaining "communion" and "spirituality," that they have no time to think about saving the world!

But God would get the whole use of you, and every minute of your time, if you knew the blessed life of being joined to the living Lord and hidden with Him in God, so that, centered in God, He holds you, and in Him you live and move and have your being.

Now for a moment pass on to Acts 2 and read it in the light of John 14:20, for, as we have seen, it is the Lord's foreshadowing of what would occur to the disciples *inwardly,* when the Holy Spirit came down and filled the house where they were sitting. God's children have been so occupied with the externalities of Pentecost—the tongues of fire and the power of utterance—that they have not sufficiently searched for light from other parts of Scripture upon the inward working of God on "that Day." The disastrous consequence of this is that many have sought for the *external* manifestations which took place at Pentecost, with no knowledge of the deep *inner life of union* foreshadowed as the inward result of the coming of the Holy Spirit "at that Day." The disciples knew, as the Spirit of God came, that Christ was GOD in very truth, that the Man they had seen go up into heaven had reached the unseen Father, and was, as He had said, "in the Father"—One with Him. VERY GOD OF VERY GOD. And they knew, as only those taught of the Holy Spirit know, that they were joined to the ascended Lord in the union of essence which is only possible to spirit, and they were one with Him in God. "One in Us" (John 17:21), said the Lord. And they knew, too, that the risen Christ, mystically, was also in them.

To perceive and experience this suddenly, *as it is possible so to do,* they must have also seen clearly the effect of the cross as the cause of this. The "baptism" they suddenly received was a *baptism into the death of Christ,* for their spirits to be released for (1) the joining with Him in His ascension life in God, and the release of their spirit to be (2) the channel of the outflow of the Holy Spirit.

Now let us pass on to the Epistles, and see whether they confirm and throw further light upon the meaning of Pentecost, and whether the ascended Lord through His revelator—Paul—reaffirms, and enlarges upon, His foreshadowing of Pentecost on the eve of His death. We have not time to fully trace this out in the Epistles. We can only turn to 1 Corinthians 12:13, where we have, in one verse again, the risen Lord's description through Paul of what took place at Pentecost. With this difference: that in John 14:20 He foreshadows the *Godward side,* and in 1 Corinthians 12:13 He emphasizes the outworking of the Spirit in and through *the Church*—the mystical Body of Christ—communicating the life and Spirit of its Head.

Let us read verses 12 and 13. "As the [natural] body is one . . . and as all the members . . . are one body, so also is Christ [*the mystical Christ, made up of Head and members*]. For in the communion of one Spirit we were all baptized [*Greek,* immersed] into one body, whether we be Jews or Gentiles, slaves or free men, and were all made to drink of the same Spirit." *The*

Speaker's Bible commentary says "*drenched* with one Spirit." The enduement of power at Pentecost is manifestly to be seen here. The context explains the way the triune God (verses 4–6) works out through the members of the Body. John 14:20 shows the believers at Pentecost in their union with the Lord taken into God; now we see the work of the Holy Spirit, forming all thus united to Christ into the spiritual organism of the Church. They were *"immersed in spirit"* according to the analogy of John the Baptist baptizing men *in water as the element.* (See the promise of Acts 1:5.) *Immersed in Spirit,* all in the upper room drank of the same Spirit, who thus produced the union foreshadowed in John 14:20.

The principal word to emphasize in 1 Corinthians 12:13 is the word *"into."* In John 14:20, Christ said "Ye in Me," and in 1 Corinthians 12:13 we find the Holy Spirit doing this work of placing believers *into* Christ, in essential union, as members of His Body. The emphasis regarding Pentecost should therefore be not on the external and incidental manifestations, but on the *internal and spiritual meaning* of the coming of the Holy Spirit, leaving to Him the external out-working "according to His will" (see 1 Corinthians 12:18).

Now let us go back to the Acts of the Apostles to see the results of the Pentecostal enduement, in some special characteristics of their service. Consider first the word "power," at Acts 1:5 (and Luke 24:49). It is in Greek *"dunamis"*—the word from which we get our English word "dynamic." This Greek word, points out a skilled

Greek scholar, means *"inherent power"*—not so much power *put forth*, as power *possessed*. It means, among other things, "ability" and *"capability."* Just as if the Lord had said to His disciples, "You are now quite incapable, but when the Holy Ghost is come, you shall be *made capable* of doing what I want you to do." But the common idea concerning the power of Pentecost is quite different to this. It is thought of as being something miraculous, accomplishing spectacular miracles through the one who obtains it! And yet it is not so. How "incapable" many are who even testify to a "baptism of power." And how "incapable" the majority of Christians are in the smallest service for God. Incapable Sunday School teachers. Incapable Bible Class leaders. Incapable workers, or no workers at all. And often it is because these "incapable" souls think that a "baptism of power" means miraculous gifts, and not God just making them "capable" in the work for Him that lies close to their hand. The "miraculous gifts" may be given, but only so far as needed for increased "capability."

Now, using the word "power" as being made "capable" or "effective" for doing the will of God in any aspect of life or service, let us think (1) of the power of *effective utterance.* Peter was given this so that there were three thousand souls pricked to the heart through his first sermon. What an amount of teaching and preaching exists, even of gospel truth, that is ineffective and carries no weight! It has, as one has said, no "carrying power." It does not go any further than those who hear it. Watch how dependent many preachers and teachers are on their "Notes," but look at Peter, and observe how he was made "capable" of wielding the Word of God. See how the texts of the Old Testament came to him, and how he "combined" spiritual things with spiritual. He could not have "thought out" in his own mind such a comprehensive panoramic survey of the scriptures concerning Christ and put them into such a condensed form. He was given, by his immersion in the Spirit, a clarified mind, a quickened memory, and "made capable" of being God's messenger on that wonderful day; *i.e.,* he was not merely a "mouthpiece" but an intelligent co-worker with God.

Then notice (2) the characteristic of the enduement of power in *boldness of testimony.* You may have a message of vital truth, but if you are "timid" and self-conscious in giving it out, it is not effective. There must be, in giving God's message, an accent of bold certainty. We are not to be positive over any *"view"* of truth, but about *what God says.* Our business is to declare the Word of God, not "views" of it. You can be "bold" over this, for the Holy Spirit will co-witness with your declaration of "Thus saith the Lord."

And (3) *the enduement of power is needed for business.* See Acts 6:3: "Look ye out seven men of honest report, full of the Holy Ghost and wisdom, that we may appoint over this business." This applies to your own "business," as well as the "business" of the Church, if your "business" is in the will of God for you. We read that David became "skillful in business" after he had received the anointing. A businessman in London said to me once, "You do not know very much about business, but you do the very things unconsciously that would be accounted the highest wisdom in business!" Yes, *the Holy Spirit knows "business,"* and can guide you so that you have no muddle in your business affairs. I was once speaking with a man of business about the opportunities he had in his particular business to do great things for the kingdom of God, but he replied, "That is all right, but I have to get my bread and butter!" But the Lord will see that you get the "bread and butter" if you seek first the kingdom of God in your earthly affairs. Alas, alas, how the devil is entangling Christian businessmen today, so as to paralyze them in the work of God and destroy their influence. Why should we call "preaching" a greater thing than "business"? Does it not depend upon what is the plan of God for you?

Then there is (4) *the enduement of power as manifested in the ordinary life.* "Be filled with the indwelling of the Spirit when you speak to one another . . ." (Ephesians 5:18–19). Here we have *effective conversation,* so that God uses you in all your daily contacts with others. Then we find power given for "contending for the faith." Paul increased in strength for "confounding the Jews" as he sought to prove to them that Jesus was the Christ (Acts 9:22). (See also Acts 7, concerning Stephen.) Controversy must not be shirked when it is necessary for the maintenance of truth. Truth must never be sacrificed for peace. Stephen and Paul were both endued with power for this work.

Then (5) there is the *being made capable to meet satanic powers.* This we see in the story of Paul and the sorcerer Elymas (Acts 13). When the apostles met this man and Satan withstood them, Paul steadily resisted him and rebuked the demon in him, just as he did later the girl with the spirit of divination. The apostle, in the second case, did not speak in a moment. He bore with the poor deceived soul until the influx of the Spirit of God arose in his spirit.

If you are centered in God, and walking with Him, you will find, too, that as you come against the power of darkness in some specific way, the Spirit of God will at the right moment rise in you in divine strength to deal with it. Paul knew the moment to turn round upon the demon and say, *"I command thee in the name of Jesus Christ to come out of her."*

Notice (6) the *"discernment of spirits"* which Paul had. He discerned the evil spirit in the girl, and in the sorcerer. This is not the "gift" of perception, or discernment, but power to tell the difference between "spirits." Our time will not allow more, but you can see in 1 Corinthians 12 the working of the Holy Spirit in the members of the Body of Christ, making one and the other "capable" for the carrying out of the will of God.

In conclusion, let us go back to the cross as the basis of all that we have spoken of. Let us turn now from our union with Christ in His life, and the enduement of power by immersion in the Holy Spirit, to see once more the place of the cross in the work of the Spirit, in carrying out all those purposes of God.

In 1 Corinthians 12:13 we read, "*By one Spirit* are we all baptized into one body whether we be Jews or Gentiles. . . ." Jews and Gentiles, we read in Ephesians 2:14, had a "wall of partition" between them. How could they both become members of Christ's Mystical Body, and be made to "drink of one Spirit"? *Only through the cross.* Therefore the cross stands as the basis of John 14:20 and Acts 2. The cross lies at the base of the UNITY OF THE BODY, and only so far as the deep work of the cross is known can the members of the Body be welded together in the drinking of one Spirit. Let us read Ephesians 2:13–17. "Now, *in Christ Jesus,* ye, who were once far off, have been brought near through the blood of Christ. For He is our peace, who has made both one, and has broken down the wall which parted us; for, in His flesh, He destroyed the ground of our enmity . . . that He might create *in Himself* one new man; and that, BY HIS CROSS, He might reconcile both, in one body, unto God, having slain their enmity thereby."

The *place* of unity between Christians today is clearly *the cross.* And this by its destroying all ground of enmity between those for whom Christ died. Between Jew and Gentile the barrier was that of "ordinances." But crucified with Christ, the "Jew" ceases to be a Jew, the "Gentile" ceases to be a Gentile. And, shall we say, the "Baptist" ceases to be a Baptist, the "Wesleyan" a

Wesleyan, and so on. All these externalities may exist, and be conformed to, but they belong to the external life only, because each regenerate believer is inwardly a member of the Body of Christ, part of a New Creation, which is neither Jew nor Gentile, male nor female, but a "New Man" consisting of Christ the Head of His members.

It is very important that in practice God's children understand the two positions: externally the earthly position, with earthly relationships; and inwardly the heavenly position in Christ. Here in this Conference, we are neither Wesleyans nor Baptists nor Church of England, nor Jews, nor Gentiles. We are all one in Christ Jesus. But when, for example, one goes back to his own sphere, he is a Baptist Minister, loyal and faithful to his section of the Church. We need to remember the heavenly position, and *when to act according to it;* and the home or business position, and when to act in harmony with it. For example, in your heavenly position you may be a leader, even though in your "home" position you may be a "subordinate." Today the Church of God needs to set an example of law-abiding faithfulness. "Lawlessness" is abroad. Servants unfit to lead are seeking to be "masters." And "masters" are failing in leadership also, showing themselves unworthy of the name. The word "servant" is being cast aside as something derogatory. It is for the Church to lift it again to its place of dignity. We should be "kings" in our heavenly position, and *on earth* the *servants* of all. We do not have ideal churches today, and so the path is difficult, but let us remember that God is a God of order, and His children must not become a perpetual cause of disturbance in their homes or their churches.

THE CROSS IS THE PLACE OF UNITY, because there the old Adam-life in the Jew and the Gentile is crucified, and God created a "new man" in Christ Jesus. How the cross breaks down the old Adam-life in its "wall of partition," dividing Christian from Christian. I once was in a conference near Berlin, Germany. Leading Christian workers had gathered from every part of Germany for a three-day conference. At the first meeting I gave a message, by translation, on the subject of the cross as set forth in Ephesians 2. On this occasion I spoke a sentence, then quietly waited, and listened while the German was given, the pauses rendering the message more effective—until suddenly a sister arose from the audience and said something in German. I waited. Then she turned and directed her words to someone at the back, and this person arose and began to shake hands with another person. Then I saw that God was working and taking hold of the meeting. So I sat and watched, and had no further opportunity to speak. The whole of the conference proceeded to settle up affairs with one another. The weeping and the "reconciliations" were most touching. The result was that after an hour or so of this blessed evidence of the power of the cross to "slay" the "enmity" between children of God, the conference broke up and away went the workers in the woods around, some of them arm in arm with those they had not spoken to for years. After this we truly had a floodtide of blessing. The "fire of the Lord" fell. We continued on the theme of the cross from one aspect and another, until we reached the point where we might safely seek the enduement for service. More than half of those present came forward and flung themselves down by the platform, asking God that there and then there should come into their spirits the true influx of the Holy Spirit. *And He came.*

In every place that some of these workers went to from that conference, they had revival. In village after village, and even in the deaconess houses they were staying in for the night, it broke out. God had really come down! This proves that the Holy Spirit *needs unity between believers* before He can work, and that this real unity comes *through the cross!*

8

THE CROSS AND THE TONGUE

*"I tell you even weeping . . . [of] enemies of
the cross"*
Philippians 3:18

THE degree of our real identification with
Christ in His death, and the criterion of the
stage of our growth into the maturity of the life
of the new creation, is in no respect more
marked than in relation to the "sins of the
tongue," especially in regard to those we see to be
"enemies of the cross," ignorantly or willfully.
For in no manifestation of the "flesh" is its
activity more painful and disastrous than in
the *language used by even true servants of God*
concerning those who are either caught in the
apostasy of today, "denying the Lord that
bought them" (2 Peter 2:1), or ensnared in the
wiles of Satan in any form.

"If any stumbleth not in word, the same is a
perfect man, able to bridle the whole body also"
(James 3:2, RV), writes the Apostle James. The

word "perfect" in this passage, according to *Young's Analytical Concordance*, means "complete"—a complete man. The same word is used in Ephesians 4:13, and is rendered in the RV text as "a full-grown man"; and again in Colossians 1:28, where it is rendered by Conybeare as "full-grown in Christ"—the word denoting "grown to the ripeness of maturity." Again, we find the word in Colossians 4:12, and here it is rendered by Conybeare as meaning "ripeness of understanding, and full assurance of belief." And, lastly, the word occurs in Philippians 3:15, where the apostle writes: "Let us all, then, who are 'ripe in understanding,' be thus minded . . ."—the word "perfect" being the antithesis of "babe" (Conybeare's note).

According to the Apostle James, then, stumbling not in word is the supreme mark of a "complete" spiritual man, completely "full-grown in Christ," having come to the ripeness of maturity as a new creature in Christ Jesus, thus having "ripeness of understanding and full assurance of belief"—being no longer a child "tossed to and fro, and carried about by every wind of doctrine, by the sleight of men . . . after the wiles of error" (Ephesians 4:14, RV), but able to speak the truth in love, in the full assurance of faith, and in calm, ripe knowledge of maturity in Christ.

The present is a sifting time for all the children of God in every degree in the spiritual life. "Spiritual" men now will prove their "ripeness of maturity" by their "stumbling not in word" during the present distress. Panic and hasty, unloving words cannot be coexistent with the "full assurance of faith" and the deep knowledge of God of the truly "spiritual" man. The spirit of the man who is "ripe in understanding" is shown in the words of Paul immediately following his utterance, "Let us who are 'perfect' be thus minded." "Many walk," he says, "of whom I told you often, and now tell you *even weeping*, that they are the enemies of the cross of Christ . . ." (Philippians 3:18). "Even weeping!" Ah! *this is the spirit of the spiritual man!* No man who weeps in speaking of the enemies of the cross will "stumble in word" and grieve the Holy Spirit of God by the fruit of his lips. The truth must be spoken—but in *love*, and with "anguish of heart and many tears" (2 Corinthians 2:4), for those who have gone astray. And let us not forget that the "truth" means not what we consider "truth" about another, but bearing witness to the truth of God as "it is written," and as we have proved and known it in our lives.

And to "stumble not in word" has much to do with our power in prayer, and our abiding in the place where we can have power with God and prevail with men. If the adversary can draw us out of the hidden place "with Christ in God" into the strife of tongues, he will do it. Prayer warriors, let us take heed that we abide in the place where we can "lift up holy hands without wrath and doubting." We must "stumble not in word" if we are to be truly abiding within the veil.

And why? The Apostle James clearly shows the reason: "Doth the fountain send forth from the same opening sweet water and bitter?"

(James 3:11). Can we speak words—bitter words—one moment, and the very next be a channel for the sweet, pure stream of the "river of water of life, clear as crystal, proceeding out of the Throne of God and the Lamb"? Let us listen again to James, and hear him tell the reason why the mark of a man truly "sanctified" in spirit, soul and body is the "stumbling not in word."

"The tongue," says the apostle, "setteth on fire the wheel of nature [or birth, RV, mg.], and is set on fire by hell." The "wheel of nature," or the life which came to us from the first Adam in our birth into this world, is always roused or "fired" by hell—by the Serpent which poisoned the stream of the earth-born life in Eden. And the Serpent's most effectual weapon is the tongue, for "firing" the "wheel of nature" in ourselves or others. Hence the wondrous silence manifested by Christ—the Last Adam—as the pattern of the Christ-life for His redeemed, when He was accused by the chief priests and elders. *He answered nothing.* "Then saith Pilate unto Him, Hearest Thou not how many things they witness against Thee? And He gave him no answer, not even to one word: insomuch that the governor marveled greatly." Only when appealed to for truth did the Lord Christ speak and bear witness to the truth (see John 18:37). "Art Thou a king, then?" said Pilate. "Thou sayest it, because I am a king" (RV, mg.), replied the Kingly Prisoner.

Even so must it be today. *Silence from witness-bearing is criminal.* The trumpet voices of the leaders of God's spiritual Israel must give no uncertain sound in the day of battle, but in all ranks of the army of the Lord "the wheel of nature" must not be fired by hell, or it will be disaster indeed. The wheel—or movement—of the life of nature which came to us at birth must be *kept continually under the power of the cross of Christ* so that the life of the Last Adam may grow in us into ripeness of maturity. The soul who has thus been united to Christ in *death* knows how to "always" bear about the dying of Jesus, and to hide in the Cleft of the Rock away from the strife of tongues, which "hell" would use to "fire" the old life, were it not *kept crucified* with Christ.

The mark, therefore, of a full-grown spiritual man as "stumbling not in word" is now easy to be understood. He has become "full-grown" with his body under the complete mastery of the Spirit. The "deadly poison" of the Serpent transmitted by the tongue to rouse "the wheel of nature" must find the believer hidden deep in the death of the cross, so that he becomes a channel for God to speak through him with healing, blessing, life-giving words of love. Let us therefore take heed at this time and ask for the light of God upon the words of our mouth, lest we lose unwittingly our power within the veil. Let us "take forth the precious from the vile"—*i.e.*, distinguish in the light of God what words are from Him and what are of our own mind, so that we may be as His mouth (Jeremiah 15:19) in this day of crisis.

9

THE CROSS AND REVIVAL

IF we look back at the messages of the preceding meetings we can see why revival comes into view at this juncture. In the Revival in Wales the outstanding theme was the message of Calvary. It is only when we see the *cross* as the center, and the basis of all the working of the Holy Spirit, that revival becomes possible. Let us now seek to understand some of the laws and *perils* of revival even when we know something of the various aspects of the cross. In dealing with this subject I will embody matter from a manuscript which was intended to form part of the last chapter of *War on the Saints*, and for some cause it was omitted. It has its origin in lessons learned in the Revival in Wales.

First let us define briefly that *revival, in its essence, is the outflow of the Spirit of God through the human spirit.*

This is in harmony with what Fausset, the well-known evangelical commentator, says about the human spirit. He writes, *"The spirit of man is the receptacle of the Holy Spirit, and is the organ in which He dwells, and through which He works."* You will see, by this simple definition, how vitally all the truths of the cross, and the laws of the spiritual life, which we have been considering, affect the question of "revival."

Now let us ask, What are the primary conditions for revival, apart from prayer? *First, the negative:* the removal of all obstacles to the outflow of the Spirit. This brings in the work of the cross applied by the Spirit of God.

Second, the positive: understanding how to cooperate with the Holy Spirit of God. This brings in the life-side of the cross, the inflow of the Holy Spirit and the believer learning experientially how to walk in the spirit.

Now as to some of the main "obstacles." (1) In the *spirit*—an unbending, unforgiving, grasping spirit. (2) In the *life*—ignorance of what is right and what is wrong, so that things which hinder the Holy Spirit are tolerated. (3) In the *service of God*—unwillingness to speak of the things of God, and to testify.

For dealing with the obstacles is needed: (1) *The cleansing of the spirit* (2 Corinthians 7:1), by the putting away of unyieldedness; the forgiving of those who have trespassed against us; the surrender of a "grasping" spirit by giving up all to God. (2) *The seeking of light from God* upon "right" and "wrong" in the life, and the putting right of things as the light is given. (3) *The surrender to God* for obedience to the directives of the Holy Spirit in the way of speech and testimony. The believer is given the blood to cleanse all that the light reveals, and the cross in its delivering power, setting him free by his identification with Christ in His death, applied by the Holy Spirit.

Now *as to the perils of revival:* These again may be briefly defined as, (1) the danger of acting or living by "feeling," or the sensuous life, instead of the spirit-life; and (2) the peril arising from the spirits of evil counterfeiting the workings of the Holy Spirit. Alongside of the danger of becoming dominated by "feelings" and emotions, the perils of revival come mainly from the invisible world of spirits. The Counterfeiter is watching to counterfeit, and to insert his workings in the place of God's workings. The fact became clear again and again in Wales, during the height of the 1905 Revival, that it was possible for God to *begin* with a pure work of the Holy Spirit and for the counterfeiting spirits to later insert a "counterfeit" which the soul ignorantly accepted. In this way the same manifestations appeared, but the *source* was changed without it being detected. The changing of the *source* of the supernatural manifestations without the believer's awareness is therefore the main peril. A very small inserted "stream" or "tincture" from the enemy causes mixture which may not be discerned at first, but which sooner or later produces fruit in confusion and trouble.

In view of this danger—the principal danger—if we pray for revival we should pray God to prepare intelligent and spiritually equipped children of God to guide and help His people: believers who know the ways of God, and who know the ways of the enemy, and are really endued by God with the power of discerning spirits—able to tell at once when the source of spiritual phenomena is changed. Such souls can discern when the spirit working in a meeting is changed from pure to counterfeit, and know how to deal with the spurious spirit and to bring the gathering back again into the pure stream of God. This occurred in the Revival in Wales many times, and those who watched the leadership of the one who was thus "discerning" the spirits at work, marveled.

I recollect once being in a meeting in England where the atmosphere was as pure as crystal. The spirit-sense, when it knows God, can *sense atmosphere*, and where God is in great power there is a sense of the "terrible crystal" Ezekiel spoke about. It then seems as if the atmosphere is so transparent that everything in it out of harmony with God seems repulsive and painful. The atmosphere of the meeting referred to was like this, when one who was present rose to pray, and immediately it seemed as if a muddy stream was poured into the meeting, filling the atmosphere with a sense of "thickness," and the pure and beautiful clearly crystal sense of the Holy Presence of God was gone. That soul had prayed from the *sensuous* soulish life and not from the spirit.

Those who have this acute and sensitive consciousness of what is "spirit" and what is "soul"— or sensuous—can *detect it in themselves* by the sound of the voice, which becomes "metallic" or harsh when the believer draws upon his "natural" resources, but when he speaks from the spirit there is an exquisite softness and purity in the voice, which makes the tone beautiful. Ah yes, everything that comes from the Spirit of God is beautiful. There is nothing repulsive—nothing that you would shrink away from—so beware of forcing yourself to accept, as of God, what your spirit shrinks from as repulsive. So many today are being drawn into counterfeits because they do not remember this. Let us have a right conception of God's presence. Where He is in power you get a foretaste of heaven, and this heavenly presence is felt *by your spirit*, not your soul, *i.e.*, your physical consciousness. "God is a Spirit, and they that worship Him must worship Him in spirit and in truth."

Alas, that so many today should be deceived as to their true spiritual state, by the effort made in many churches to appeal to the sensuous, and the natural love of the beautiful, through beautiful music and attractive singing—which will count for nothing in eternity. If it is true that "God is a Spirit, and they that worship Him must *worship Him in spirit,*" of what avail is all the sensuous worship caused through the soothing or satiating of soul-desires, with no real knowledge of God or His gospel. Let us see to it ourselves that our worship of God is in spirit, and in truth.

As we have seen, the chief peril of revival is that when God begins to work in abnormal power, the Counterfeiter has his opportunity. It is then that what a writer in America calls "the high order spirits," the religious spirits, that "hover upon the Alps of the spiritual life," hover about those who are entering realms of the spirit they have never known before. Not the gross and repulsive spirits, but refined and beautiful spirits, are the ones most to be feared. When Paul said that Satan had transformed himself into an "angel of light," he plainly meant that Satan can appear to be *light* when he himself is all darkness. He can give "flashes of light" and "floods of light," and fill a room with light. Can *you* tell when they are from the enemy?

All that we have been learning about the cross will equip us to meet these "perils." Therefore if we pray for and desire revival, we must ask God to enable us to apprehend the truths that will fit us to be of use to Him when it comes.

Now lastly, let us summarize some hints on how to conduct meetings to bring about revival, or during an existing time of revival—a time when the Spirit of God is working in great power. These "hints" are adaptable, though revival—true revival—cannot be worked up by methods. These hints are offered only to show how to co-work with the Holy Spirit on the right occasion, so as to give Him full liberty to work.

We have seen that "revival" is the result of an influx into and an outflow from the regenerated human spirit. The baptism of the Holy Spirit, or the enduement of power, therefore brings into *acute consciousness the spirit-sense,* which, if we learn to read it correctly, will teach us how to work with the Holy Spirit in the conducting of a meeting, not only as He moves through our own spirit, but as He moves in the spirit of others.

1. *First, as to the leader of the meeting:* The leader should be one chosen of God, and equipped by the power of the Holy Spirit. He must therefore be:

(a) Baptized with the Spirit, so that he is conscious of the spirit-sense referred to, whereby he knows the mind of the Spirit in himself and is able to discern it in others.

(b) The leader, thus open to the leading of the Holy Spirit, should be able to speak at any moment as the need arises—free from dependence on notes or aids to memory. To guide the meeting under the guidance of the Spirit, he needs to be able to speak "as the Spirit gives utterance," and to know the right moment and the right message.

(c) The leader must never let go the reins of the meeting—leading throughout, even though he may outwardly appear to be taking no part at all.

May I illustrate the importance of this by a concrete example. I was once attending a huge gathering where one who had been greatly used in revival in another land was present, and the meeting was given over to him. He spoke just a few words. Then, placing his watch upon the desk, he bowed his head in prayer, and deliberately let go the meeting as if he had nothing to do with it. It could be seen that he had taken his hands right off it. That is, he did not continue to *inwardly* hold it *by watching and being ready to intervene.* The result was startling. The moment he "let go" inwardly, there was a wild outburst from a section of that meeting place which was indescribable. There was a "hissing" as if serpents were there, and a wailing noise like the whistling of the wind in the rigging of a ship in a storm. But the leader did not attempt to deal with this, and there was no regaining of the control of that gathering—it was practically wrecked. No work of God could be done in that atmosphere. This shows that when God gives charge of a meeting to anyone, *he is responsible to hold it for God,* and to rely upon the Holy Spirit in directly quenching any inroads of the spirits of Satan. No one could pretend that the outburst I have described was of God.

(d) The leader must *keenly watch the meeting,* seeking, in reliance upon God, discernment as to when to touch it (outwardly) and when to leave it alone; and when to move with God in song or prayer or message.

2. *Second, as to the meeting:* A program based on a prearranged plan is no hindrance, for it can be used if there is no discernable movement of the Holy Spirit among the people. But the leader must be ready to drop the "program" when the Spirit of God shows him to do so. However, the meeting should not be allowed to "take its own course" until the Holy Spirit is undoubtedly at work among the people.

We saw this today in the Prayer Conference. There was a blessed working of the Holy Spirit, and He was in control. The last quarter of an hour, all who prayed, prayed in the spirit. It is a great sign that the Holy Spirit is in control when people are "condensed" and to the point, with no garrulousness of the "flesh." It is the atmosphere that is the great thing. When God is fully in control you will find that the meeting will need very little guiding by the leader.

The intrusion of fleshly activity at any point should at once be dealt with. This can be done by taking the meeting to prayer, or by the leader speaking. The "flesh" must never be allowed to take control of a meeting, even though it may break in for a brief period. The leader should watch how to check it and eliminate its effects by some Spirit-guided course of action.

The leader should also be on guard and keenly ready to discern any breaking out of evil spirits, who are always watching to insert their own stream when there is any movement by God. By the discerning of spirits, which is given with the enduement of power, a leader who knows the life after the Spirit can detect the first trace of the working of the enemy. He need not tell the people of this, but by prayer, or a message of truth, or silent resistance (in spirit) he can quickly extinguish their workings.

3. *Third, how to get a "heavy" meeting into liberty.*

(a) The "burdens" on all present may first be removed by asking for audible prayer or expressions of need.

People go to a meeting burdened with their own troubles, and with their spirits crushed or weighted. Burdened in spirit, they are not open to God because they are burdened. The leader begins to speak to them, and think them "so hard." But they are not "hard"—*they are burdened.* It would probably "liberate" the meeting if at first all could be free to express their burdens, either in prayer or by asking for prayer by others.

(b) The leader should take *time* to get the meeting free. When it is free from weight, pressure, heaviness, he will find it easy to give the message.

(c) The leader should *be in victory himself*, so that he is able to lift the meeting and not be dependent upon the people for his own liberation. Sometimes the speaker himself goes to a meeting burdened, trusting for inspiration to come to him from the meeting. But that is not God's way. The speaker should not be dependent upon the response of the people, but be able to change the atmosphere and bring the gathering into liberty; *i.e.*, the meeting should not be used as a "crutch" to make up for lack of prayer and preparation, or to liberate the speaker from his own burden.

(d) The speaker should give his message even if he is conscious of opposition to the truth he is giving, either in the atmosphere—from the powers of darkness—or by the people, and as he does so the Holy Spirit will work and the meeting will be *mastered by the truth*, thus forestalling the devil, who will otherwise get a hold upon it.

We have been talking about an enduement of power that is *effective*, and there is a degree of the power of God working through us which would conquer any meeting. The secret of it lies in the "grain-of-wheat" life, for when the believer is deeply immersed in the death of Christ, there is an outflow of the Holy Spirit which, as it were, soaks the meeting—as if it were soaked in an overflow of the river of life flowing from the Throne of God. It is something more than the individual getting of blessing. However much we may know of God's working through us already, there must be possible a stronger, purer force of the divine Spirit in our spirits if we learn more deeply the conditions of the working of His power.

In any case, it would always be best for the speaker not to put down "hard" meetings to the state of the people, but to look upon such "hardness" as a deeper call to the cross for himself, and to the "grain-of-wheat" experience of fellowship with Christ.

(e) All in the meeting should understand they are free to take part, and there should be no tie to time. The meeting should be free to go on until it is evident that the Spirit of God would have its conclusion. This is one of the greatest needs in "revival," but very difficult circumstantially to obtain. Yet so often when the Spirit of God has been at the highest point of working, it has been necessary to close the meeting. Only God can show His servants how this point can be met. May He teach us how to work with Him in revival power.

Note: The question may be asked whether, in view of the Lord's return, we are to pray for, or *expect*, revival. There is, undoubtedly, at the present time an awakening of prayer for "revival," for the conviction is growing that the only alternative to "revolution" is "revival"—*or the Lord's coming.* The history of the French Revolution, and how England was saved from a similar upheaval by the revival through Wesley, is referred to by many, and it is historically true that again and again when England seemed as much in the dark as darkest Africa, God intervened in answer to the cry of His people.

But "THE COMING OF THE LORD DRAWETH NIGH." Whether "revival" will precede that glorious event or follow it, we do not know. The Apostle Peter's word at Pentecost, that the outpouring then given was only an *earnest* of the fulfillment of Joel's prophecy for the latter days, is sufficient to show that "revival" is now due, whether it comes before or as a result of the Lord's coming. In either case we can pray for it, and prepare the way for it, whether we shall be in it, or out of it by being "absent from the body and present with the Lord."

10

THE CROSS AS A
PROCLAMATION

"THE word of the cross is the *dunamis* of God," said the Apostle Paul. Dr. Mabie points out that the Greek word here is *logos*, or word—not *preaching*, as in the King James Version. It is the same word used of Christ Himself in John 1:1: "In the beginning was the *Logos*, and the *Logos* was with God, and the *Logos* was God." The Greek Lexicon gives the meaning of *logos* as (1) The word by which the inward thought is expressed, and (2) the inward thought itself. Christ the Son of God *in Himself* is God's "Word" to the world—His "inward thought" expressed (Hebrews 1:3); and He is God's inward thought itself clothed in terms of humanity. The "logos" of the cross is also God's "inward thought expressed" of the only way in which He could save fallen man and recreate him in the image of Christ. The logos of the cross therefore contains *in itself* the power of God. It is dynamic—and through it the Holy

Spirit manifests the energizing ability of God to save. It is not the *"preaching"* of the cross which is the power, but the *word* of the cross, and it is this "word of the cross" which is to be proclaimed to a fallen and lost world, as a message from God, announced as a herald ANNOUNCES A PROCLAMATION by an earthly king.

This can be traced out in the Epistles of Paul. *"I proclaimed* to you," he said, "the message which I bore" (1 Thessalonians 2:9). Conybeare's footnote says, "The original word involves the idea of a herald proclaiming a message." Again in Titus 1:3: "He made known His word in due season, in the message [lit. *proclamation*] committed to my trust by the command of God our Saviour." And Galatians 1:16: "When it pleased Him . . . to reveal His Son in me, that *I might proclaim His glad tidings."*

A "proclamation" requires a "herald," so the apostle writes to Timothy: "The glad tidings, whereunto *I was appointed herald"* (2 Timothy 1:11). "Christ Jesus, who gave Himself a ransom for all men, to be testified to in due time. And of this testimony I was appointed herald" (1 Timothy 2:6–7). All these passages show the "herald" nature of Paul's preaching of the cross.

Now as to *the terms of the proclamation.* It is (1) the proclamation of THE CROSS: "The Jews require a sign, and the Greeks demand philosophy; but we proclaim a *Messiah crucified,* to the Jews a stumbling block and to the Greeks a folly . . ." (1 Corinthians 1:22–23); and (2) this word of the cross has its twin-truth, THE RESURRECTION: "Remember that Jesus Christ, of the seed of David, is *raised from the dead,* according to the Glad Tidings which I *proclaim*" (2 Timothy 2:8). Here we have the two-fold message of the cross stated as the terms of the proclamation. (1) A Messiah crucified, and (2) a Messiah raised from the dead. Calvary and the resurrection. Not one without the other. A real physical death and a real physical resurrection.

Then as to *the responsibility of the herald to proclaim the message.* We find this in 1 Corinthians 9:16, where Paul writes about himself: "Although I *proclaim* the glad tidings, this gives me no ground of boasting; for I am compelled to do so by order of my Master. Yes, woe is me if I proclaim it not. For were my service of my own free choice, I might claim wages to reward my labor; but since I serve by compulsion, I am a slave, entrusted with a stewardship." This is strong language, but Paul uses it to show the Corinthians the divine compulsion upon him and how solemn the trust committed to him. They understood in those days how absolutely a slave had to obey his master. Although the apostle served of his own free will, yet as concerning his message, the constraint upon him put him in the same place as a slave. He felt that he might not even do his work primarily for "wages"! *He had to fulfill his trust* whether he had wages or not.

Oh that this same sense of being constrained by God to "herald" His message might take hold of each of His redeemed ones, producing that white-heat fire within which makes them reckless about themselves, so long as they fulfill their stewardship. God will see to it that you get your "wages." "No man goes to warfare at his own charges." God is a poor master and a strange king if He sends out His heralds without being able to provide for them. But God *is* a King— sending out a "proclamation" to the world—and He *sees to the supplies* of those He truly sends. It often looks like madness to believe this, but the madness of really trusting God is the highest wisdom. *"I proclaim"* because *"I am compelled,"* said the apostle.

Next, *as to the place of the proclamation in relation to other truth.* "Christ sent me forth as His apostle, not to baptize, *but to publish the glad tidings"* (1 Corinthians 1:17). The external ordinances were secondary in importance to the proclamation of the message. In the mission field, therefore, the primary work of the missionaries is not to get so many heathen "baptized" and entered on a church roll, but to publish the glad tidings.

And *as to the language and the way in which the proclamation is to be given.* "Not with wisdom of word, lest thereby the cross of Christ shall be made void." The proclamation does not need the adornment of beautiful words and the oratorical display of language. It has only to be *proclaimed* in its bare simplicity, for it is the "word" of the cross which is the power of God, not words about it. Here is stated also the solemn fact that the message which contains the mighty power of God can be rendered "void," or powerless, by the preacher. The words which the natural man in his human wisdom thinks are necessary to make the message acceptable have actually the contrary result, in making void the power of the cross itself. This explains why today there is so little result even when the true gospel is preached. *So few really believe that the "word" itself, simply stated, has in it the "power of God."* They are not willing to be simple transmitters of the written Word. They want to preach "sermons" *about* the cross—rather than simply PROCLAIM it!

How did Paul fulfill his commission, as a "herald" with a "proclamation"? "When I came among you, and declared to you the testimony of God, I came not with surpassing skill of speech, or wisdom. For no knowledge did I purpose to display among you, but the knowledge of Jesus Christ alone, and Him—*crucified*" (1 Corinthians 2:1-2). And then he adds, "In my intercourse with you, I was *filled with weakness.*" Oh Paul, have you not mistaken the word? Did you not mean that you were filled with power? No. "I was filled with *weakness,* and fear and much trembling." Conybeare's footnote points out that this peculiarly Pauline expression means a "trembling anxiety to perform a duty." The "anxious conscientiousness" of a "slave."

When the solemnity of the trust and the vital character of the message of the cross is realized by anyone, it is bound to produce that "trembling anxiety" lest he should fail God, or become unfitted for the Holy Spirit to use him with the message. *"And when I proclaimed my message,"* the apostle continues, "I did use not *persuasive words of human wisdom,* but showed forth the working of God's Spirit and power, that your faith might have its foundation not in the wisdom of men, but in the power of God." Here it is again. Paul deliberately avoiding using "persuasive words." Human influence and "persuasion" is not needed in addition to the "power of God." The herald simply has to be carefully exact in transmitting the proclamation. Then the responsibility is with God, and those who hear it. Is it not strange to be using words all about the things of earth to draw men to God, instead of simply heralding forth God's proclamation?

What about the urgency of the proclamation? How Paul labored to prepare Timothy to carry on the work when he knew that his departure was at hand. Listen to his last solemn words to him: "I adjure thee before God and Jesus Christ . . . *proclaim* the tidings, be urgent in season and out of season, convince, rebuke, exhort, with all forbearance and perseverance in teaching. For a time will come when they will not endure the sound doctrine, but according to their own inclinations, they will heap up for themselves teachers upon teachers to please their itching ears. And they will turn away their ears from the truth, and turn aside to fables." So the aged Paul was under no misconception as to the attitude of many to the truth of the gospel after he had gone—especially in the latter days in which we are now living. Nevertheless, "I adjure thee . . . PROCLAIM" is written to us as well as to Timothy.

The passion of his message was in Paul to the very end. The one thing he cared about was his stewardship. When he looks back upon his sufferings, all is swallowed up in the fact that he had accomplished his ministry. "When I was first heard in my defence, no man stood by me, but all forsook me; (I pray that it may not be laid to their charge). Nevertheless, the Lord Jesus stood by me, and strengthened my heart, that by me *the proclamation of the glad tidings* might be accomplished in full measure, and that all the Gentiles might hear; and I was delivered out of the lion's mouth" (2 Timothy 4:16–17), he writes.

Let us finally *take a glimpse into the inner life of the apostle* so that the *spirit* of it may get into us and urge us forward to "proclaim" the message of the cross with new perception of its urgency and its power. The apostle's words to the elders at Miletus show us vividly the spirit of his labors. "Brethren, ye know yourselves . . . after what manner I have been with you throughout the time; serving the Lord Jesus with all lowliness of mind, and with many tears and trials which befell me through the plotting of the Jews. And how I kept back none of those things which are profitable to you. . . . And now, as for me, behold I go to Jerusalem, in spirit foredoomed to chains; yet I know not the things which shall befall me there, save that in every city the Holy Spirit gives the same testimony, that bonds and afflictions await me. But none of these things move me, neither count I my life dear unto myself, so that I might finish my course with joy, and the ministry which I received from the Lord Jesus to *testify the glad tidings*" (Acts 20:18–24).

In 2 Corinthians 6:4–10, we have a glimpse into his service as a herald. *"I commend myself as one who ministers to God's service;* in steadfast endurance, in afflictions, in necessities, in stripes, in imprisonments, . . . as ever dying, yet behold I live; as chastened by suffering, yet not destroyed; as sorrowful, yet ever filled with joy; as poor, yet making many rich." Then in 2 Corinthians 4 we see how he handled the Word of God. He said, "I have renounced the secret dealings of shame, I walk not in the paths of cunning, I *adulterate not the Word of God: but openly setting forth the truth,* as in the sight of God, *I commend myself to the conscience of all men."* Keen as Paul was to win souls to Christ, he used no cunning schemes to reach them. Oh the dishonorable things that are done to get hold of converts, or "members" for a church! Many are disguised under the idea of lawful "guile" or "wisdom" for the reaching of the people. But Paul boldly depended upon an open, straightforward *proclamation of the word of the cross,* believing it to be the "power of God." He "openly set forth the truth" in such a way that the consciences of men were reached, both by the plain, honest statement of his message and the transparent clearness of his life.

All that is *of God* can be openly proclaimed to all. There are no degrees of "initiation" in the Church of God. There are different stages of *growth* in knowledge, but no "secret truths" which cannot be proclaimed to the whole world. Oh for this bold, straightforward, open declaration of the Word of God, relying upon it as the power of God. May we all be saved from cunning scheming under the guise of "making known the truth." There should be no "sheep-stealing," no "proselytizing," and no "planning" to get hold of this one and that one. Let us openly proclaim God's message in the simple terms of the Scriptures, assured of the co-working of God.

The apostasy of the visible church can alone be countered by the proclamation of the word of the cross, with the spirit of the apostle and *in the way Paul proclaimed it.* Is the "apostasy" among the people in the pews, *or is it in the pulpits?* Will God condemn the "sheep" or the "shepherds" charged with feeding the flock? Those who have to face the people who sit under the apostasy of the pulpit, and afresh lift up the banner of the cross, need to get a new faith and a fresh vision from God. Then consider the *way* in which the gospel of the cross should be proclaimed. Let us ask why there is so much apparent preaching of the gospel which has so little result. *Is there something wrong about the way in which it is presented?* Some time ago when I was pondering over this, a leaflet came into my hands in which the writer said that the great need today was that souls should be invited to "come to the risen Lord." And then I saw the weakness in this way of preaching the gospel. Let me put it as a question to those who are preachers and teachers. Is the gospel of the cross to be proclaimed thus: The Lord Christ died instead of sinners on Calvary, and having completed the work of redemption, He went back to heaven; and now His messengers, on the ground of what He did at Calvary, are to *call sinners to the risen Christ?* Or it is an absolute necessity that *the Holy Spirit should make Christ's death at Calvary* so real to *each sinner* who needs salvation, that they realize first His *death* for them, and *then* come to Him as a living Saviour?

The first method practically eliminates the cross. For thousands of people "come to Christ" who do not realize at all the fact of *His death* for them. The result is that many of these souls give *little evidence of regeneration*—they are not radically changed and made new creatures in Christ.

There is a subtle and strange omission of the preaching of the cross because of this emphasis upon the risen Lord. He *is* the living Saviour, but we do not come to Him only through His merits, or even on the ground of His work at Calvary—but *that death on Calvary must be made real to us by the Holy Spirit,* so that we see *our* part in it, and know that we are born into a new life through His death as our Substitute.

Galatians 3:1 emphasizes this in a very vivid way. "Oh senseless Galatians, who has bewitched you?" writes the apostle. "You, before whose eyes was held up the picture of Jesus Christ upon the cross." This is the literal sense, says Conybeare, and Lightfoot uses the word *"placarded."* This was the way Paul preached. He *"proclaimed"* the "word of the cross as the power of God" and he "placarded" Jesus Christ upon His cross before the Galatians, so that, as it were, they saw the crucifixion with their very eyes. This is the message to be proclaimed, just as if you went out as a herald, saying, "A proclamation from heaven: He was lifted up on the cross for *you.* BEHOLD THE LAMB OF GOD!"

Then lastly, a "herald" does not proclaim his message in a feeble voice, or in a timid self-conscious way! Let us not fear to lift up the voice like a trumpet. *The trumpet that God uses now* is the voice of one who will be a herald and messenger, saying, "Behold the Lamb of God, which beareth away the sin of the world."

APPENDIX

THE CROSS AND THE
BLOOD COMPARED

Note: The following summary of texts showing the *difference* between the experiential application of "the cross" and the application of "the blood" to the believer is given to make clear that when the Word speaks of one it does not mean the other.

THE CROSS OF CALVARY

I. *The Place of Sin-bearing by the Substitute.*
   1. He "bare our sins . . . on the tree, that we, being dead to sins, should live unto righteousness. . . ."

                                (1 Peter 2:24)

   2. The place of reconciliation: ". . . reconciled by His death. . . ."

                                (Romans 5:10)

II. *The Place of the "Sinner" Crucified.*
   1. Our "old man crucified with Him . . . that henceforth . . . not serve sin"

                                (Romans 6:6)

   2. "I . . . crucified with Christ . . . not I

but Christ liveth in me. . . ."

(Galatians 2:20)

3. "They that are Christ's have crucified the flesh. . . ."

(Galatians 5:24)

4. "The world . . . crucified to me. . . ."

(Galatians 6:14)

III. *The Place of Unity Between Believers.*

"Reconcile both . . . by the cross, having slain the enmity thereby. . . ."

(Ephesians 2:16)

IV. *The Place of the Overthrow of Satan.*

"Principalities and powers, He made a show of . . . triumphing over them . . ." [*i.e.,* through the cross]

(Colossians 2:15)

(See John 12:31; 16:11)

V. *The Death of the Cross Applied to the Believer.*

"We who *died.* . . ."

(Romans 6:2, RV)

"Discharged . . . *having died.*"

(Romans 7:6, RV)

"Ye *died* with Christ. . . ."

(Colossians 2:20, RV)

"For *ye died.* . . ."

(Colossians 3:3, RV, mg.)

"For if *we died* with Him, we shall also live. . . ."

(2 Timothy 2:11, RV)

VI. *The Death of the "Substitute" the Death of the Sinner.*

"One died for all, therefore all *died.* . . ."

(2 Corinthians 5:14, RV)

VII. *The Continuity of the "Cross" for Every Believer as well as the Continued Application of the Blood.*

"Always delivered unto *death* . . . that the life also of Jesus manifest might be made manifest in our mortal flesh. So then death worketh in us, but LIFE in *you.* . . ."

(2 Corinthians 4:10–12;
1 Peter 1:19)

THE PRECIOUS BLOOD OF CHRIST

I. *The Outpoured Blood.*
   1. As propitiation

(Romans 3:25)

   2. As redemption
(1 Peter 1:19; Ephesians 1:7)

   3. As a "purchase" price

(Acts 20:28)

   4. As the ground of peace

(Colossians 1:20)

   5. As the ground of "justification"; *i.e.,* the sinner declared guiltless

(Romans 5:9)

II. *The Blood Within the Veil.*
   1. Christ entered through the blood

(Hebrews 9:12)
(See Hebrews 9:7; 9:22)

   2. Believers have access by the blood

(Hebrews 10:19)

   3. Believers are "made nigh by the blood of Christ"

(Ephesians 2:13)

III. *The Blood Applied to the Believer.*
   1. The type of "sprinkling" for remission

of sin

(Hebrews 9:18–23)

(See also Hebrews 12:22–24)

2. The blood to the conscience

(Hebrews 9:14)

(See also Hebrews 10:22)

3. The blood "sanctifying" or setting apart for God

(Hebrews 13:12)

4. The blood of the covenant the ground of God's work in the soul

(Hebrews 13:20–21)

5. ". . . loosed us from our sins in His blood. . . ."

(Revelation 1:5, RV, mg.)

IV. *The Condition for the Perpetual Application of the Blood.*

"If we walk in the light, as He is in the light, we have fellowship one with another, and the blood of Jesus, His Son, cleanseth us from all sin. . . ."

(1 John 1:7)

V. *The Blood of the Lamb Applied by the Spirit of God, the Weapon of Victory over Satan.*

"They overcame him by the blood of the Lamb, and by the word of their testimony; and they loved not their lives unto the death. . . ."

(Revelation 12:11)

Particulars of the magazine *The Overcomer* may be obtained from:

The Overcomer Literature Trust
9–11 Clothier Road
Brislington, Bristol BS4 5RL
England

This book was produced by the Christian Literature Crusade. We hope it has been helpful to you in living the Christian life. CLC is a literature mission with ministry in over 45 countries worldwide. If you would like to know more about us, or are interested in opportunities to serve with a faith mission, we invite you to write to:

Christian Literature Crusade
P.O. Box 1449
Fort Washington, PA 19034